CIVIL SIGHTS

# CIVIL SIGHTS

# SWEET AUBURN

## A JOURNEY THROUGH ATLANTA'S NATIONAL TREASURE

GENE KANSAS
ILLUSTRATED BY CLAY KININGHAM

Published in association with Georgia Humanities

The University of Georgia Press
Athens

This publication is made possible in part through a grant
from the Bradley Hale Fund for Southern Studies.

Published by the University of Georgia Press
Athens, Georgia 30602
www.ugapress.org

Designed by Brian Simons
Edited by J. Trevor Williams
Set in 10/13 Goudy National
Printed and bound by Versa Press
The paper in this book meets the guidelines for
permanence and durability of the Committee on
Production Guidelines for Book Longevity of the
Council on Library Resources.

Most University of Georgia Press titles are
available from popular e-book vendors.

Printed in the United States of America
28 27 26 25 P 5 4 3

EU Authorized Representative
Easy Access System Europe—Mustamäe tee 50, 10621
Tallinn, Estonia, gpsr.requests@easproject.com

Library of Congress Cataloging-in-Publication Data
Names: Kansas, Gene, author. | Kiningham, Clay, illustrator.
Title: Civil Sights: Sweet Auburn, a journey through Atlanta's national
treasure / Gene Kansas.
Description: Athens : The University of Georgia Press, [2025] | Includes
bibliographical references and index.
Identifiers: LCCN 2024028321 | ISBN 9780820367705 (paperback) |
ISBN 9780820367712 (epub) | ISBN 9780820367729 (pdf)
Subjects: LCSH: King, Martin Luther, Jr., 1929–1968—Homes and
haunts—Georgia—Atlanta. | Sweet Auburn Historic District (Atlanta,
Ga.)—Guidebooks. | Sweet Auburn Historic District (Atlanta, Ga.)—
Description and travel. | Atlanta (Ga.)—History.
Classification: LCC F294.A86 S94 2025 | DDC 917.58/23104—dc23/
eng/20240723
LC record available at https://lccn.loc.gov/2024028321

**SPECIAL THANKS TO OUR PRESERVATION PARTNERS**

Atlanta Preservation Center • The Georgia Trust for Historic Preservation • National Trust for Historic Preservation • Atlanta History Center • Global Atlanta • Georgia Humanities • Auburn Avenue Research Library • Arnall Golden Gregory LLP • Constellations
Gene Kansas | Commercial Real Estate

*Civil Sights* is dedicated to Sweet Auburn and to the preservation of its history and culture.

# Contents

# Foreword

**GARY M. POMERANTZ**

I have heard that if you go to the great battlefield in Gettysburg, Pennsylvania, and put your ear to the ground, you can hear the distant rumble of cannons.

That sound is the resonance of history.

The truth is that to hear history—I mean, really *hear* it—you must listen for it. You must have a feel for it, a connection. Then you must reach out to it. You must go to the places where history broke out, cut loose your imagination, and hop into a time-transport machine.

Gene Kansas—writer, preservationist, and cultural developer—is in love with history. With *Civil Sights: Sweet Auburn*, Kansas has given us more than a guidebook: he's given us a gift. Because Sweet Auburn isn't just another neighborhood any more than the Reverend Dr. Martin Luther King Jr. was just another minister. King was born and raised on Auburn Avenue, and his father and grandfather were pastors at Ebenezer Baptist Church on this historic street.

Once upon a time, in the days of segregation, there were two Atlantas—White Atlanta and Black Atlanta. Auburn Avenue, part of the latter, featured a powerful sense of racial community and hope. Sweet Auburn was the commercial and spiritual hub of Black Atlanta. A certain magic resided there, especially in that two-block stretch between Piedmont Avenue and Butler Street. To walk the avenue on any summer day or evening was to experience the vitality of Black life in this city: the churches and small businesses, the nightclubs, barbershops, and shoeshine stands, especially between the Rucker Building and the Yates & Milton Drugstore. Some folks called Auburn the Black Peachtree, a mirror of White Atlanta's main commercial street.

John Wesley Dobbs—a railway mail clerk, son of enslaved persons from Cobb County, and grand master of the Prince Hall Masons of Georgia—evocatively called the avenue Sweet Auburn, in honor of the timeless Oliver Goldsmith poem from 1770, "The Deserted Village" (see the appendix).

Money made Auburn sweet, Dobbs said, and voter registration—The Ballot!—would make it even sweeter.

We know this history. But do we *hear* it?

With *Civil Sights*, Kansas takes us to Sweet Auburn, and with his well-researched stories, he allows us to put our ears to the ground and listen.

In chapter 4, you'll hear the sweet sounds of Bessie Smith, Cab Calloway, and Louis Armstrong coming from the Royal Peacock nightclub.

Then on Sunday morning—the church hour—you'll hear the Auburn Avenue ministers, the Reverend Martin Luther King Sr. (aka Daddy King) at Ebenezer, and the Reverend William Holmes Borders at Wheat Street Baptist Church, quoting Scripture and delivering sermons.

That resonant voice you'll hear in chapter 3 belongs to Dobbs, known to his Masons as the Grand. Walking along the avenue, Dobbs, a race man, takes off his fedora, hands it to a bystander, and quotes Shakespeare, Du Bois, and Francis Bacon, imploring listeners to understand that the way to true freedom for Black Georgians is through bucks, ballots, and books.

In chapter 3, you'll also hear the singing voices of the brotherhood of the Prince Hall Masons in the Masonic Lodge—the same building where, on the first floor, Martin Luther King Jr. planted the headquarters for his civil rights organization, the Southern Christian Leadership Conference. In chapter 4, you'll hear newsboys down the street calling out headlines in front of the building housing the *Atlanta Daily World*, founded in 1928 as the nation's first twentieth-century African American daily.

Make no mistake, along Auburn Avenue—powerfully and profoundly—history marched and marches still.

Big moments, small moments: in *Civil Sights*, Gene Kansas gives them all to us.

Listen!

# Acknowledgments


## IN CULTURAL AND CREATIVE PARTNERSHIP

This book represents a labor of love. I have profound appreciation for collaborators and friends to history Clay Kiningham, J. Trevor Williams, Molly Slavin, Ellen Goldlust, Jon Davies, Brian Simons, Helen McGaughy, Jason Orme, Jonathan Lawrence, Anuj Desai, Michelle Davis, and Matt Wilson, all of whom contributed meaningfully to the mission. To my good friend Gary M. Pomerantz, I am honored you chose to write the foreword to *Civil Sights* and feel a great sense of pride in your support. To Jacqueline Jones Royster, I am forever thankful for your invaluable mentorship, your insight into and memories about Sweet Auburn, and your beautiful afterword. I am also exceptionally thankful to the University of Georgia Press for believing in *Civil Sights* and particularly to Editor-in-Chief Nate Holly, a dedicated and thoughtful partner who has helped bring out the best in us all.

## WITH LOVE

I owe my great love for history, culture, and community to my wonderfully encouraging parents and grandparents, to my adventurous and fun-loving sister, to the societal gumbo of New Orleans I was fortunate to experience growing up, and to the historic and contemporary opportunities the great city of Atlanta continues to provide. I am a lucky man to have had Sam, Emma, and Miss D raise me as family, helping me become the person I am today. And I am quite blessed to share my personal history and love for life with my wife, DeAnna, and son, Levi, for their cherished support, hugs, and healthy motivation all along the way. For all, I am incredibly grateful.

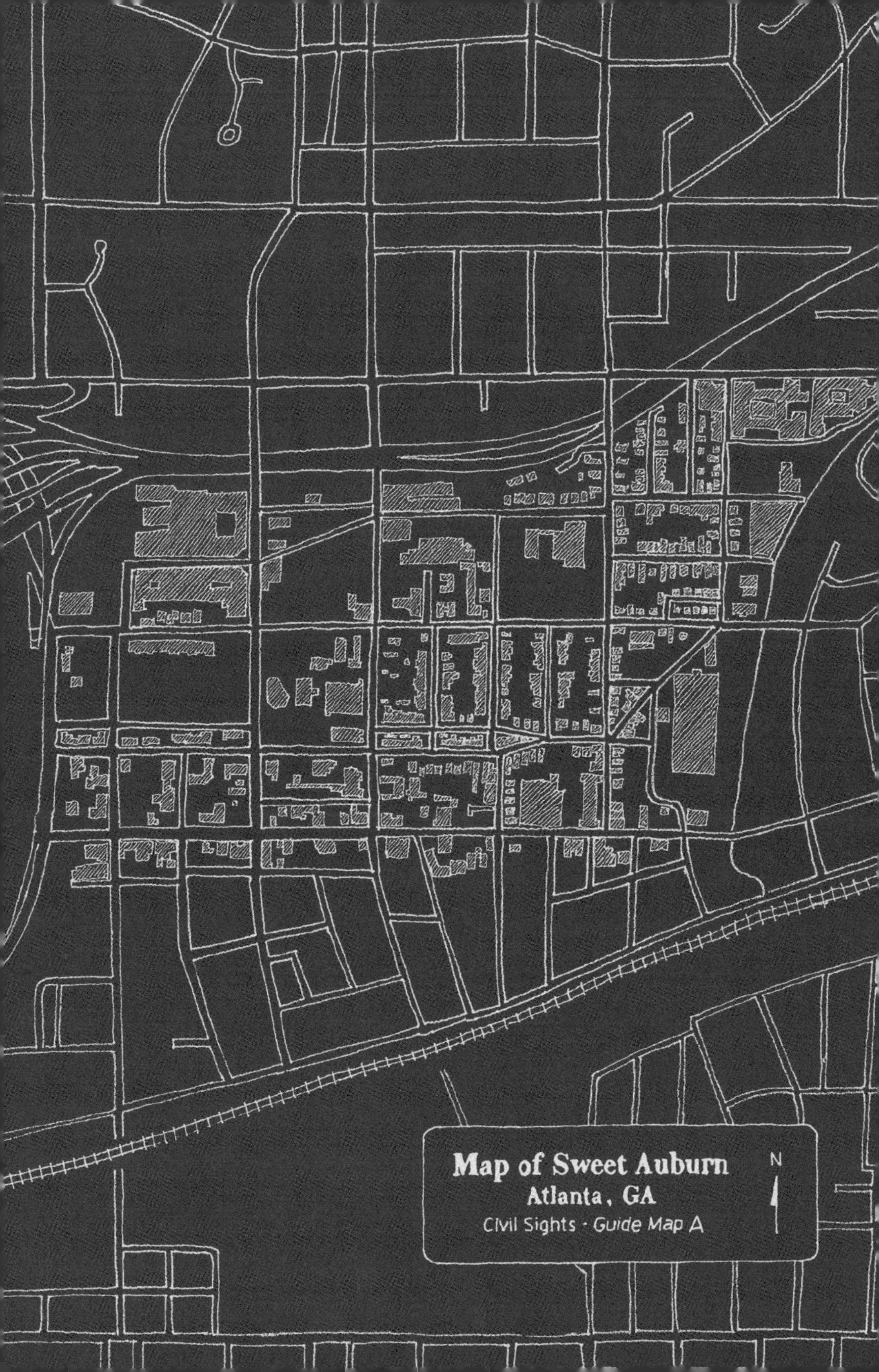
Map of Sweet Auburn
Atlanta, GA
Civil Sights · Guide Map A
N

# CIVIL SIGHTS

"THE ETERNAL FLAME SYMBOLIZES THE CONTINUING EFFORT TO REALIZE DR. KING'S IDEALS FOR THE 'BELOVED COMMUNITY' WHICH REQUIRES LASTING PERSONAL COMMITMENT THAT CANNOT WEAKEN WHEN FACED WITH OBSTACLES."

THE ETERNAL FLAME AND HISTORIC MARKER AT THE GRAVESITE OF MARTIN LUTHER KING JR., AT THE KING CENTER IN ATLANTA, GA

# Introduction

## MISSION OF THE GUIDE

In 1854, less than a decade before the onset of the American Civil War, a free Black woman named Laura Lavinia (Kelly) Combs purchased a small lot at the intersection of Whitehall Street (now Peachtree) and Wheat Street (now Auburn Avenue). With this visionary acquisition, Combs became the first Black person to own property in Sweet Auburn, a district later recognized as the primary nexus of Black culture and commerce in the United States despite extreme challenges in the face of institutionalized segregation. In a move foreshadowing the neighborhood's ethos of empowerment, Combs soon directed her investment toward a profound and deeply personal mission, exchanging that land for something of far greater value: her husband's freedom from slavery.

Despite his acquired freedom, John Combs was of course still held captive by the laws of the segregationist South. As you'll painfully read in chapter 2's section on the Cox Brothers Funeral Home, many contemporaries believed that only through death could Black people truly be free. Until passage of the Civil Rights Act of 1964, which prohibited discrimination based on race, color, religion, sex, or national origin, millions of Black men, women, and children remained legally subjugated. Over time and with considerable sacrifice, extraordinary progress has been made, and yet much work remains to be done.

Laura Combs was among the first in Sweet Auburn to guide us, to lead the way, to demonstrate what's possible. Now, 170 years later, fortitude, vision, and action are needed once again to safeguard this sacred neighborhood, a national treasure that is home to the birthplace of Dr. Martin Luther King Jr. and the Civil Rights Movement as well as a place of provenance for so many other important people and organizations. Their work and the vital lessons they provided are at stake, as is the tenuous fate of our future.

In 1976, the secretary of the interior designated this internationally significant neighborhood as a National Historic Landmark District. Since then, however, 47 percent of its historic buildings have been lost. This tragic yet preventable forfeiture of history carries amplified relevance today amid heightened calls for justice focused on civil and human rights across our city, state, and country.

Sweet Auburn faces an untenable irony, at once globally appreciated yet locally hanging in the balance as Atlanta grows in, around, and over it. The neighborhood has twice been named to the National Trust for Historic Preservation's Endangered List (1992, 2012) and twice listed among the Georgia Trust for Historic Preservation's "Places in Peril" (2006, 2013). Regrettably, little meaningful progress has occurred since the early 2010s. Without urgent action toward preservation, more buildings will crumble, burn, or face the wrecking ball. If we lose this physical context, we may lose our way, and future generations will never learn the historical lessons that the buildings and fabric of Sweet Auburn are ideally suited to teach by virtue of their ability to connect people to place through the lives and accomplishments of those who came before us.

It has been said that history does not repeat itself: rather, people repeat it by failing to learn from prior experiences. No one can re-create the past, but by preserving it with a sense of forward-thinking creativity and renewed vigor, it is possible to better navigate an uncertain future.

Enter *Civil Sights: Sweet Auburn*, a guide that not only describes and depicts buildings and streets but also tells the stories of people and places, then and now, that came together to move mountains. Guides, by definition, help show the way, and this book illuminates a path to preservation by taking the reader on a historic journey through a community whose powerful blend of faith, education, entrepreneurship, and activism sparked a nonviolent revolution that activated a nation's conscience and vastly improved the world.

This book demonstrates the symbiotic relationship between people and place and ultimately how we identify with ourselves, with our communities, and with each other for common good. As a writer turned preservationist and cultural developer, I now primarily share stories through the built environment, a medium characterized by buildings, spaces, and places that constitute cities, encourage culture, and provide both backdrops and stages for history to be made. Given my professional commitments and personal love for Sweet Auburn, I naturally desired a deeper understanding of the interconnected networks of awe-inspiring people who inhabited the buildings, homes, and businesses that lend the neighborhood its sense of place.

FLAT IRON BUILDING
AT THE INTERSECTION OF
PEACHTREE AND SWEET AUBURN

To supplement their stories, *Civil Sights* also interweaves a sketchbook by architect Clay Kiningham that chronicles both the beauty and the flaws of this neighborhood in this moment in time, an artful reminder of just how delicate a line we are all walking.

For many people, a visit to Sweet Auburn is monumental and identity-defining. It's a rite of passage—a chance for inspiration, contemplation, and consideration, with the potential to act as a turning point. This book could never provide a comprehensive history of Sweet Auburn, whose residents' achievements fill volumes on their own. But it can seed conversations about how much of an impact we can make on the world, individually and collectively, and about the consequences of our actions—and inactions.

In this way, *Civil Sights* issues both an invitation and a challenge. Yes, we highlight moments of levity, places to eat, and worlds to explore, but we also describe structures that through their continued and sometimes neglected existence pose questions of historical accountability to us all. How are we educating about, advocating for, and investing in the causes that Sweet Auburn represents?

By sharing this content and context, readers will gain a deeper connection to this historic neighborhood. The deeper these connections, the more value we assign to the place and, in turn, the more motivated we become to conserve, protect, and care for it. This action, inspired by passion rather than obligation, is a necessary ingredient for the positive and thoughtful change that is needed in Sweet Auburn, not as a means of re-creating its past but to preserve it as a platform of inspiration and activism for future generations.

Yet as we contemplate this call to past and present, we must also logically observe the world is ever changing. Even as I type, spaces and places in Sweet Auburn are being constructed and falling apart; others are well on their way toward deliberate demolition. *Civil Sights: Sweet Auburn* offers but a snapshot in time, chronicling through words and sketches how the neighborhood overtly and quietly stands at the onset of 2024. These pages will help to fix in time and memory moments of great pride, progress, and work to be done.

Perhaps along your journey, you will cross paths and join hands with kindred travelers from across the city or around the world. Such interactions and the visionary collaborations we hope they inspire are just what *our* historic district needs. The future of our history is not a foregone conclusion. We must take an active role in helping to save it. By being here, you're already contributing to its preservation.

Y·M·C·A

# What Is a Sketchbook?

**CLAY KININGHAM**

Stated simply, a sketchbook is a book full of rough drawings and notes. It is done to understand ideas and surroundings through drawing as little or as much detail as necessary. Whether places and scenes are inspiring because of their historic significance, quirks, small details, lighting, or undefined impressions, a sketch is done to see truly and accurately those details that are inspiring. Unlike a photograph, which extracts all visual details in an instant, a sketch pinpoints the most inspiring and necessary details. To sketch is to be in dialogue with one's surroundings, understanding and seeing in the most intimate way. To keep a sketchbook is to make a habit of sketching for the purpose of understanding and seeing, and the result is a book that can be treasured and shared.

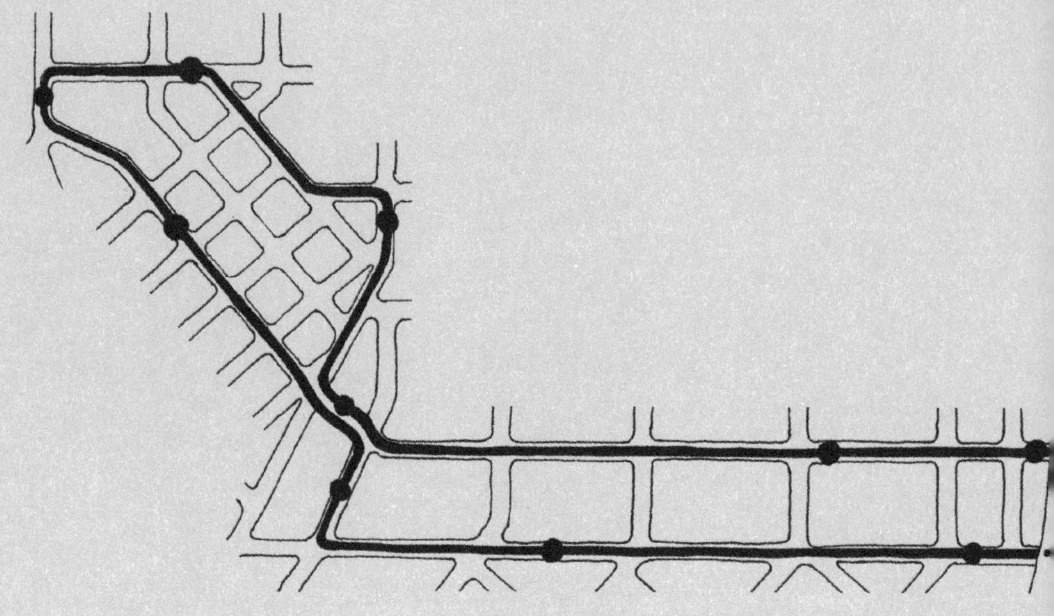

# Your Guide to the Atlanta Streetcar

The Atlanta Streetcar runs along a 2.7-mile route between the King Center and Centennial Olympic Park, providing a convenient way to travel and sightsee in Sweet Auburn. With twelve stops, there's plenty to see along the way. Places of interest featured in *Civil Sights* are listed on each chapter title page, accompanied by an Atlanta Streetcar map to help readers—and riders—navigate their journey. Enjoy!

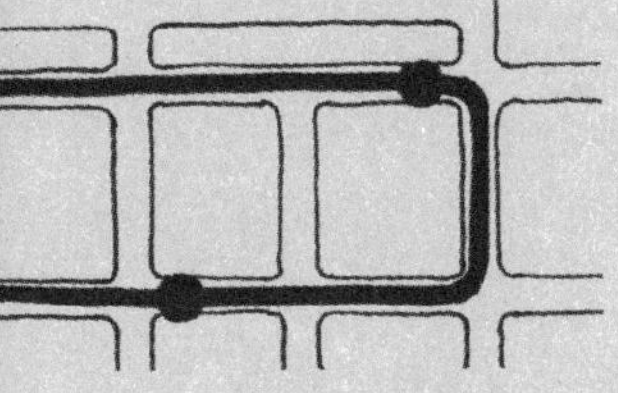

ATLANTA STREETCAR STOPS

- AUBURN AT PIEDMONT
- CARNEGIE AT SPRING
- CENTENNIAL OLYMPIC PARK
- DOBBS PLAZA
- EDGEWOOD AT HILLIARD
- HURT PARK
- KING HISTORIC DISTRICT
- LUCKIE AT CONE
- PARK PLACE
- PEACHTREE CENTER
- SWEET AUBURN MARKET
- WOODRUFF PARK

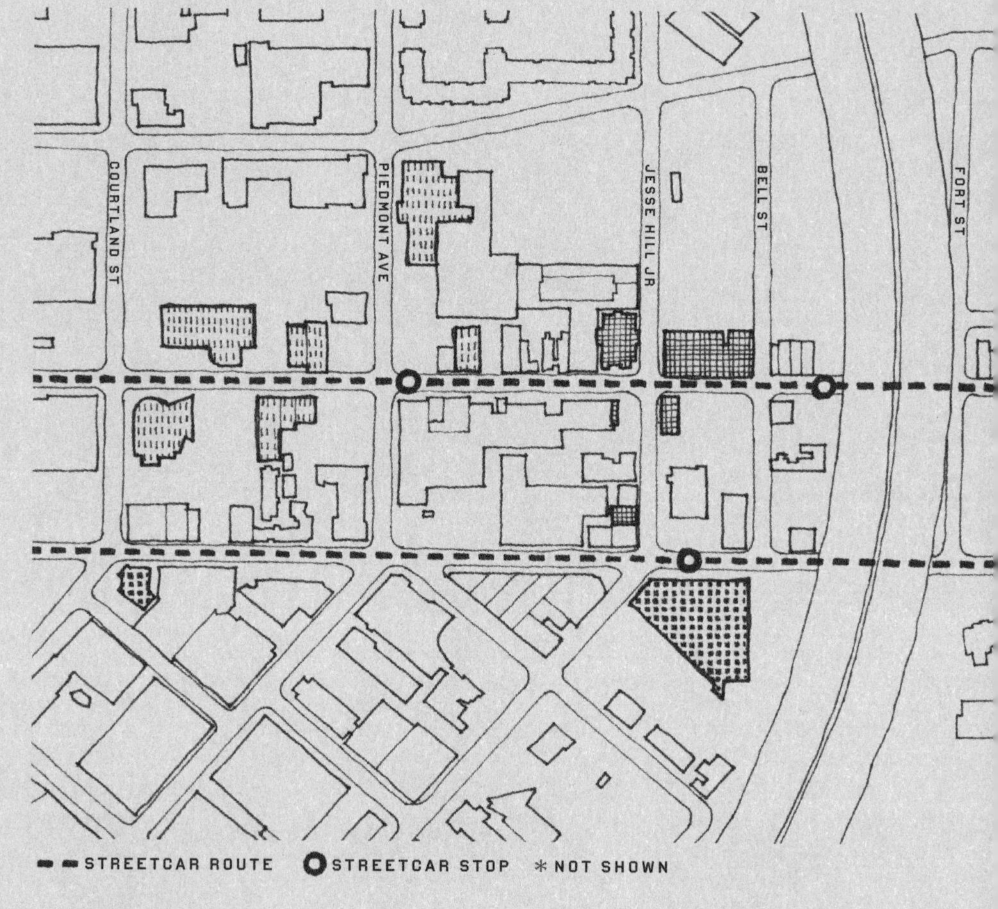


## 1 THE BIRTH HOME BLOCK

**MARTIN LUTHER KING JR. BIRTH HOME**
501 AUBURN

**CHARLES LINCOLN HARPER HOUSE**
535 AUBURN

**HAMILTON HOWELL HOUSE**
102 HOWELL

**BRYANT-GRAVES HOUSE**
522 AUBURN

**SHOTGUN ROW HOUSES**
472-488 AUBURN

**FIRE STATION NO. 6**
37-39 BOULEVARD

## 2 MLK

**THE KING CENTER**
449 AUBURN

**OUR LADY OF LOURDES**
25-29 BOULEVARD

**EBENEZER BAPTIST CHURCH**
407 AUBURN

**COX BROTHERS FUNERAL HOME**
380 AUBURN

**WHEAT STREET BAPTIST CHURCH**
359 AUBURN

**SOUTHERN CHRISTIAN LEADERSHIP CONFERENCE (SCLC)**
330 AUBURN

## 3 DOBBS

**THE PRINCE HALL MASONIC LODGE**
330 AUBURN

**JOHN WESLEY DOBBS PLAZA**
AUBURN AT FORT STREET

**ODD FELLOWS BUILDING AND ANNEX**
228-250 AUBURN

**GOLD DUST TWINS AND THE ATLANTA LIFE LOCAL BRANCH**
229-243 AUBURN

**BIG BETHEL AFRICAN METHODIST EPISCOPAL (AME) CHURCH**
220 AUBURN

**JOHN LEWIS HERO MURAL**
AUBURN AND JESSE HILL

**BUTLER STREET YMCA**
22 JESSE HILL JR. DR

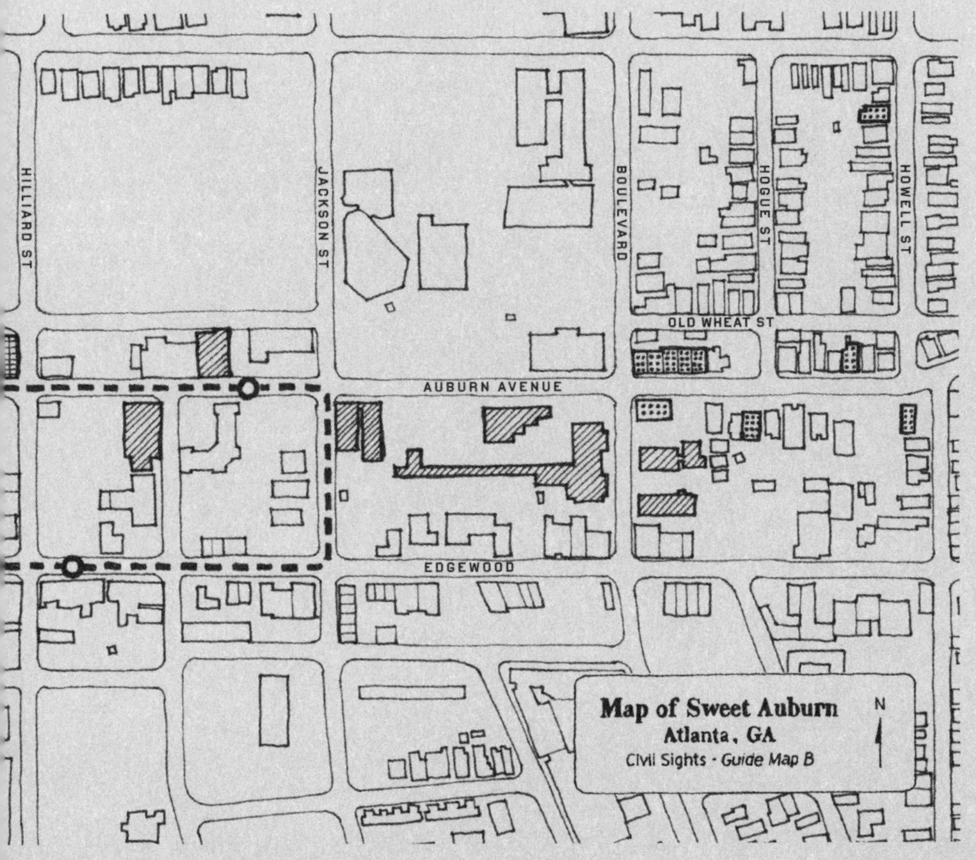


## 4 AUBURN AT PIEDMONT

**THE ROYAL PEACOCK**
186 AUBURN

**CITIZENS TRUST BANK**
75 PIEDMONT

***ATLANTA DAILY WORLD* BUILDING**
145 AUBURN

**100 BLACK MEN OF AMERICA**
141 AUBURN

**ATLANTA LIFE INSURANCE COMPANY**
142-148 AUBURN

**SOUTHERN SCHOOL BOOK BUILDING**
135 AUBURN

**CENTENNIAL HALL**
100 AUBURN

**AUBURN AVENUE RESEARCH LIBRARY ON AFRICAN AMERICAN CULTURE AND HISTORY**
101 AUBURN

## 5 EDGEWOOD AND DOWNTOWN

**THE CURB MARKET**
209 EDGEWOOD

**DIXIE COCA-COLA BOTTLING COMPANY PLANT**
125 EDGEWOOD

* **HERREN'S**
84 LUCKIE ST

* **NATIONAL CENTER FOR CIVIL AND HUMAN RIGHTS**
100 IVAN ALLEN

## 6 OLD FOURTH WARD

* **KING MEMORIAL MARTA STATION**
377 DECATUR

* **THE ATLANTA BELTLINE**
ACCESS FROM IRWIN STREET NE

* **OLD FOURTH WARD WATER TOWER AND STUDIOPLEX**
659 AUBURN

## AN OVERVIEW

*This chapter explores the people and places of the Birth Home Block, an important ecosystem surrounding the childhood home of Martin Luther King Jr.—a home and block that imbued deep and resonant life experiences and seeds of a worldview into a prospective leader, starting him down the path toward a more just future.*

*Exploring this foundational block not only provides fundamental context for the life, influences, and outlook of* MLK *Jr. but also delivers fascinating and inspiring microbiographies of the forefathers and -mothers of the Civil Rights Movement.*

*The Birth Home Block is a fundamental experience when visiting the Martin Luther King Jr. National Historical Park, a historically and culturally rich thirty-five-acre destination administered and interpreted by the National Park Service.*

CHAPTER 1

# THE BIRTH HOME BLOCK

## *A Worldview Informed*

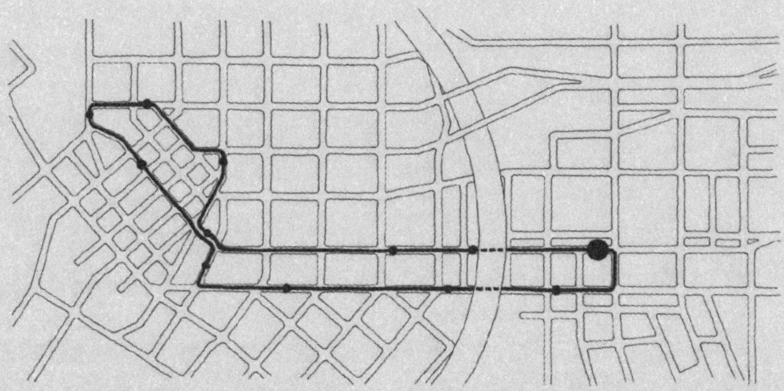

ATLANTA STREETCAR STOP: KING HISTORIC DISTRICT

**MARTIN LUTHER KING JR. BIRTH HOME**
501 AUBURN AVENUE

**CHARLES LINCOLN HARPER HOUSE**
535 AUBURN AVENUE

**HAMILTON HOWELL HOUSE**
102 HOWELL STREET

**BRYANT-GRAVES HOUSE**
522 AUBURN AVENUE

**SHOTGUN ROW HOUSES**
472–488 AUBURN AVENUE

**FIRE STATION NO. 6**
37–39 BOULEVARD

MARTIN LUTHER KING JR. BIRTH HOME
501 AUBURN AVE NE

# Martin Luther King Jr. Birth Home

**501 AUBURN AVENUE**

The Reverend Dr. Martin Luther King Jr. was born at noon on Tuesday, January 15, 1929, in an upstairs bedroom at this 1895 Queen Anne–style two-story home. Michael Jr., as he was known in those days, lived the first twelve years of his life here before the family moved to a now-demolished house a few blocks away at 193 Boulevard. For the young MLK Jr., the Birth Home and the surrounding neighborhood were simply the backdrop of his childhood: a place to play hide-and-seek, to study, and to get into mischief.

Originally built for a white family, the home was bought in 1909 by King's maternal grandfather, the Reverend Adam Daniel Williams, the second pastor of Ebenezer Baptist Church. The third pastor was Martin Luther King Jr.'s father, Daddy King, who took up the post in 1931 and whose ministry brought many activists and organizers into the family home. Walking between home and church, MLK Jr. encountered Black Atlantans of many different social classes. Seeing economic hardship and disparities up close sowed seeds that King later cultivated into a holistic worldview that insisted that true equality necessarily included economic empowerment.

Designated a National Historic Site by Congress in 1980, the Birth Home has become a mecca for tourists as well as a site of interest for those who study the origins of the Civil Rights Movement and its ongoing influence on the fight against racism. Currently closed for renovations, it is expected to reopen to the public in November 2025.

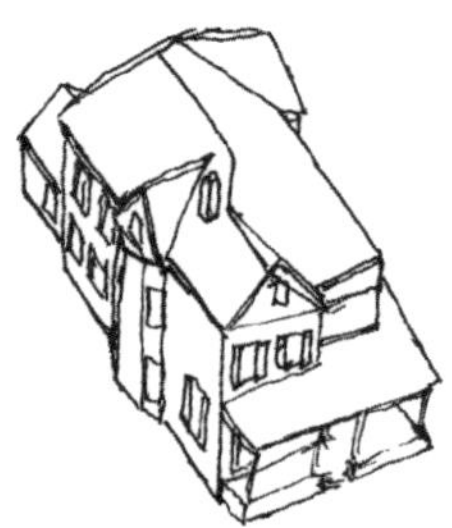

MARTIN LUTHER KING JR. BIRTH HOME

# Charles Lincoln Harper House

## 535 AUBURN AVENUE

Born in Hancock County, Georgia, in 1877, Charles Lincoln Harper bought the charming and inspirational 1895 Queen Anne–style home at 535 Auburn Avenue in 1910. He resided there for the next forty years, serving as an influential high school principal and contributing to the educational fabric that became crucial to Sweet Auburn's role in birthing the Civil Rights Movement.

The house features distinctive elements such as a stained-glass border on the front window and decorative wood-scroll details on the eaves and window surrounds. This type of ornamentation appealed to many middle-class Black families moving to Sweet Auburn in the early 1900s, and the Victorian design resembles that of the nearby MLK Jr. Birth Home and others on the street.

The impact of design in Sweet Auburn is not surprising. From Constantinople to the Roman Catholic Church and well beyond, image, identity, and upward mobility have all influenced architectural styles and symbols. Turn-of-the-century Sweet Auburn homebuyers sought to leverage conspicuous elements of success to demonstrate prosperity and enjoy a sense of pride in their accomplishments. Ornamentation informed both the distinctiveness of the Sweet Auburn home *and* the homeowner, influencing architects, builders, and neighbors alike.

Expressions of value and personalized renditions allowed for variety in Sweet Auburn and delivered visual representations of

progress for the community at large. Forward-looking architecture was of course not confined to Sweet Auburn. Social mobility was and is an aspiration of communities throughout the United States, but its promulgation through design in Sweet Auburn and the Old Fourth Ward more broadly showed what possibilities lay ahead for an inspired generation looking to rise above racial discrimination.

The National Register of Historic Places considers the Harper House and its architectural style critically significant to the historic character of the block where King was born. Included in the Martin Luther King Jr. National Historical Park, the two-story home has been continually occupied by Black residents since its construction. It is now part of the National Park Service's Historic Leasing Program, in which private entities enter into long-term leases on historic properties to add present-day vitality and to aid in preservation.

Harper attended Morris Brown College, whose high school program he later led. As an educator, he saw how books could help determine the realization of civil rights, and he believed that "America's survival depended upon a thorough education of the youth of this country without regard to race, color, or creed."[1]

As with many leaders, Harper's focus on education was entwined with religious instruction. Harper attended Big Bethel AME Church at 220 Auburn Avenue, where Morris Brown College held classes in the basement before its campus was completed. He became superintendent of the church's Sunday School.

In 1924, Harper entered his highest and most significant office when he became the inaugural principal of the Washington Park neighborhood's Booker T. Washington High School, named in honor of the author, educator, political leader and first principal of Tuskegee Institute. Before the school's establishment, Atlanta had offered Black students no public education beyond the sixth grade, and Washington High's creation thus remedied a core problem that had inhibited Harper's ambition to educate the community's young people. With his work at Washington, Harper was building on the foundation of the Neighborhood Union, an organization of the city's leading African American women led by Lugenia Burns Hope, a community activist and wife of Morehouse College president John Hope. The union had led a very long and intense campaign for a public high school for Atlanta's Black students.

By all accounts, Harper advocated tirelessly for the school and its students. He organized external tours for honors students and their families, set up a student government, and recruited well-educated teachers who cared for students' lives beyond the classroom. He displayed considerable capacity for fundraising, rallying donors in the neighborhood and beyond to purchase adjoining land for athletic fields and eventually to build a stadium. He commissioned an exact replica of Tuskegee's Booker T. Washington statue, *Lifting the Veil of Ignorance*, to be installed in front of Washington High. By the time Harper retired in 1942—the same year Martin Luther King

Jr. enrolled as a sophomore—Booker T. Washington High School's forty-two hundred students made it the largest Black high school in the United States.

Harper also founded and acted as the executive secretary of the Georgia Teachers and Education Association, the state's professional organization for Black teachers and administrators. In addition, he served as an organizer and leader in the corollary national organization, the American Teachers Association. The city named Charles Lincoln Harper High School (now closed) and a small city park on Joseph E. Lowery Boulevard in his honor.

When Harper died in 1955, Thurgood Marshall, who a year earlier had won the landmark *Brown v. Board of Education* U.S. Supreme Court decision that barred segregated education and who later became the Court's first Black justice, recognized not only Harper's effectiveness as an educator but also the tenacity such a job required in an antagonistic environment. "There have been others devoted to causes," Marshall said. "However, Professor Harper stood out head and shoulders above many others because of his complete lack of fear of physical and economic repercussions."[2]

In addition to his educational work and leadership, Harper also served as president of the Atlanta branch of the NAACP. He is buried at historic South-View Cemetery.

# Hamilton Howell House

## 102 HOWELL STREET

It's the people that make the place—in this case, quite literally. In Sweet Auburn, Alexander Hamilton (born enslaved ca. 1840) and his son Alexander D. Hamilton (born November 24, 1870) were the city's foremost Black builders of their day. Alexander Hamilton and Son was formed when the junior Hamilton joined his father's business in 1890.

According to the National Park Service, Alexander D. Hamilton built his family home at 102 Howell Street sometime between 1890 and 1895. The thoughtful design features a Palladian window on the top level and ornate Corinthian columns supporting the front porch. In 1984, the home was purchased and restored by local civic leader Mtamanika Youngblood and her husband, George Howell, who became only the second owners in the home's history. In 2017, an Invest Atlanta Community Empowerment Fund Grant helped Youngblood complete a further renovation, turning the home into a bed-and-breakfast.

Alexander Hamilton died in 1911, but the company continued operations into the 1920s. One of its more impressive projects was the 1916 construction of the Butler Street YMCA, a Sweet Auburn landmark affectionately known as Black City Hall and designed by renowned architectural firm Hentz, Reid & Adler. Another noteworthy assignment came in 1923 when Alexander Hamilton

and Son was hired to rebuild Big Bethel AME Church after a fire significantly damaged the building.

With these commissions and many other homes, schools, and community buildings, Alexander Hamilton and Son earned a reputation as a leading builder of early twentieth century Atlanta and a meaningful contributor to Sweet Auburn's evolution as an internationally recognized neighborhood representing Black wealth and culture.

A Mason, Odd Fellow, and devout Christian, Alexander D. Hamilton died in January 1944, having stated that "the most

valuable influences shaping his life were home and parents."[1] Both he and his father are buried at Oakland Cemetery.

Today, Howell Street is a pleasant mix of young and old residents, with historic homes lending charm and constancy to a neighborhood in continual transformation. A stroll down this often-overlooked street offers a sense of how the community developed and a chance to reflect on the labor and love that went into designing and maintaining it.

# Bryant-Graves House

## 522 AUBURN AVENUE

In Black communities across the country, voices of leadership were born in the pulpit and raised on the newspaper, with sermons and editorials setting stages and establishing legends. These platforms of great trust helped galvanize shared visions that turned the tides of history.

The first Black churches date back to the late 1700s, when they were founded primarily by formerly enslaved persons in Augusta and Savannah, Georgia; Philadelphia; and Petersburg, Virginia. The causes these churches supported—welfare for the needy, equity in education, housing for orphans, and mutual care through benevolent societies—helped extend a local sense of cooperation into universal concern for the well-being of all people, a central theme of the Civil Rights Movement. These Black churches' histories as places of influence positioned them as powerful institutions whose leaders could walk in both the Black and white worlds, bridging gaps in communication and culture.

Peter James Bryant was born on April 23, 1870, in Sylvania, Georgia. His parents, Inman and Caroline Moore Bryant, were born enslaved, with his father also serving as a well-respected Baptist preacher. The ministry, it seemed, was always in Peter's blood; he assisted his father in prayer meetings beginning at age eleven and became Sunday School superintendent at twelve. Just three years later, he began to preach. In May 1898, Rev. Bryant settled in Atlanta and began working as pastor at Wheat Street Baptist Church, just a few years after the Victorian-style home had been built at 522 Auburn. Wheat Street's membership rolls stood at sixteen hundred upon his arrival; at his death in 1929, the church counted more than five thousand congregants.

Bryant was not only a great orator but also an accomplished writer, supplementing his preaching with another mainstay of connected communication: the newspaper. In the Black community, the press was a vital and vibrant cultural phenomenon for many years. The first Black newspaper in the United States was *Freedom's Journal*, founded by Rev. Peter Williams Jr. and other free Black men in New York City. The inaugural issue was published on March 16, 1827, with input from founding editors John Russwurm and Samuel Cornish. Nearly eighty years later, in the unsettled wake of Reconstruction and amid the violent backlash of the Jim Crow era, Atlanta saw the founding of the *Voice of the Negro*, an Atlanta literary magazine whose first issue was published in January 1904 with national distribution. According to the opening manifesto,

> *The Voice of the Negro* for 1904 will keep you posted on Current History, Educational Improvements, Art, Science, Race Issues, Sociological Movements and Religion. It is the herald of the Dawn of the Day. It is the first magazine ever edited in the South by Colored Men. It will prove to be a necessity in the cultured colored homes and a source of information on Negro inspirations and aspirations in the white homes.[1]

Founder Austin N. Jenkins, a white manager for the J. L. Nichols publishing company, saw to it that the periodical's editorial control lay with Black founding editors John W. E. Bowen Sr. and Jesse Max Barber. Rev. Bryant served as an associate editor. Bowen and Barber desired that the magazine include "current and sociological history so accurately given and so vividly portrayed that it will become a kind of documentation for the coming generation."[2]

The *Voice of the Negro* grew louder as it attracted leading luminaries who used its pages to promote Black philosophies and political views. Contributors included W. E. B. Du Bois and Booker T. Washington, with Washington eventually holding the most significant role. His articles and commentary helped to propel him into a prominent role as the spokesman and leader of the Black community, culminating with his famous "Atlanta Compromise" speech at the International Cotton States Exposition in 1895. Likewise, Du Bois's participation aided him in the 1905 launch of the Niagara Movement, which promoted Black equality in politics and in society. But of course, nothing was equal, as events in Atlanta soon reminded anyone who might have forgotten.

The Atlanta Massacre of 1906, in which an estimated thirty Black people were killed by angry white mobs numbering in the thousands, was brutal and inflammatory. Enraged by accusations that Atlanta's Black population had started the riot, Barber wrote anonymously in the *New York World* that the white press was at fault. Once his authorship was exposed, he was threatened with arrest and fled to Chicago. Facing increasing financial and social pressure, the *Voice of the Negro* fell silent in 1907.

While short lived, Bryant's stint at the paper, along with his dedication in the pulpit, showed how these overlapping platforms could provide structural reinforcement for the social causes of the day, an ethos later reflected in iconic Sweet Auburn institutions like Ebenezer Baptist Church and the *Atlanta Daily World*.

In 1910, perhaps inspired by interactions with leading thinkers and academics of the day, Bryant and his wife, Sylvia, founded the Bryant Preparatory Institute, an adult education center housed

above a grocery store. In the cramped space, Sylvia Bryant and four others taught reading, writing, and math to as many as 175 adult students, while Peter James Bryant taught courses to up-and-coming preachers including Michael King, who in 1934 changed his name to Martin Luther King Sr. and who spent time there before joining Ebenezer as pastor.

Bryant lived at 522 Auburn until his death. A Mason, an Odd Fellow, and a Pythian, he is buried at South-View Cemetery. Sylvia, who preceded him in death, lies next to him, her headstone engraved "She Hath Done What She Could."

The house at 522 Auburn subsequently became home to another educator, Antoine Graves. Born in 1862, Graves started influencing lives at a young age, becoming the first principal of Gate City Public

School when he was just twenty-two. He was fired two years later after he refused to close the school so that students could attend a memorial parade for former Confederate president Jefferson Davis, a well-known apologist for slavery. Graves later became a leader of the Storrs School, which had been founded in 1865 as Atlanta's first school for Black pupils.

Graves rose to even broader fame as an influential real estate agent in Atlanta. The city provided a business landscape where he could further utilize his strengths in leadership to make remarkable contributions through courage, vision, perseverance, and care. Perhaps most notable among the many properties he sold is the land that today features the Georgia State Capitol. He continued to stand out by working at the Kimball Building on Atlanta's Wall Street—an otherwise white-only street. In Sweet Auburn, Graves stayed in and true to the community even as he worked to help Blacks integrate other neighborhoods on Atlanta's west side.

To honor his lifelong pursuit of liberty and leadership, the Antoine Graves Building carried his name. Built in 1965 to house senior citizens at 126 Hilliard Street, the midrise was designed by future architecture and development legend John C. Portman Jr. and was one of his first and most influential creations. The building featured an atrium, an inspired move Portman later incorporated into his Hyatt Regency Atlanta, a project that garnered international renown. When the Antoine Graves Building was slated for demolition in 2009 after sustaining tornado damage, Portman was a strong and outspoken voice for its preservation, though the structure's functional obsolescence and asbestos problems ultimately led to its demise, a loss for both history and affordable housing.

Graves's wife, Catherine Webb Graves, was the daughter of an enslaved woman, Sinai Calhoun Webb, and White Atlanta's mayor Judge William Ezzard. One of a kind even after his 1941 death, Graves is interred in Oakland Cemetery's African American section, the only soul there honored with a mausoleum.

Built ca. 1894, 522 Auburn Avenue, like many Sweet Auburn homes, suffered a period of neglect after the neighborhood's midcentury decline, but it was eventually rehabilitated by the National Park Service, initially to serve as a visitor center.

Today this two-story Queen Anne is home to the Historic District Development Corporation, which conducts work in historic preservation, new construction, and community advocacy under the leadership and stewardship of Cheneé Joseph. The house "has a hip roof with a front-facing cross gable over a cutaway bay with a jigsaw second-story panel. Decorative shingles and horseshoe-shaped vents appear in the gable end. [The] Porch has turned posts, sawn brackets, an openwork frieze, and a stick balustrade."[3]

Protecting homes like the Bryant-Graves House, imbued with a history of activism and intriguing architecture, is essential to maintaining the character of the neighborhood by providing context for a period of historical significance.

# Shotgun Row Houses

**472-488 AUBURN AVENUE**
**MARTIN LUTHER KING JR. NATIONAL HISTORICAL PARK**

Our worldviews are in part constructed by what we see modeled in the physical world. For Martin Luther King Jr., growing up in a neighborhood where the stratification of society was reflected in buildings, churches, and institutions set him off along the path toward equality and justice for all.

Down an alley just two doors west of King's birth home sit three double-shotgun row houses that provided a grounded perspective for a boy who grew up solidly middle class. Built for low-income workers, the homes were constructed in 1911–12 by Atlanta's leading Black contractor, Alexander D. Hamilton, who lived just a few blocks away at 102 Howell Street. In addition to the shotguns and his own home, Hamilton's construction company, Alexander Hamilton & Son, was responsible for other integral structures such as the Butler Street YMCA and the reconstruction of Big Bethel AME Church.

Shotgun houses are traditionally narrow, laying out front to back in a linear fashion with one open room leading to the next through a series of doorways, typically without hallways. These unique and practical homes are said to get their name because a shotgun blast fired through the front door could exit out the back without hitting anything. Functional in design, these domiciles are typically single-story, simple in their facade design, and made from wood or another inexpensive material in large supply and close at hand. Additionally,

shotgun homes can be built on small parcels of land, making them relatively inexpensive. Shotgun houses rocketed to popularity in southern U.S. cities during the 1800s and early 1900s—perhaps most notably in New Orleans—because of their utilitarian nature, affordability, and relative ease of construction.

Also known as alley houses, these homes were much smaller in stature than Sweet Auburn's surrounding Queen Anne–style single-family residences built ten years earlier for middle-class whites. As post-Reconstruction white flight out of the city center picked up throughout the twentieth century, middle-class Blacks purchased the larger homes and moved into the neighborhood. By contrast, these modest shotgun rental homes had only two rooms each and lacked indoor bathrooms and electricity until 1951. Interestingly, these houses did appropriate some Queen Anne design details such as "molded crown and drip caps, mantels and ornamental firebox surrounds, and smaller elements, including ornamented door knob escutcheon plates."[1]

Starting in the early 1900s, Sweet Auburn began to ascend on the socioeconomic ladder, paralleling the power and influence Black people were gaining in Atlanta and nationally. However, Martin Luther King Jr. was born in January 1929, less than a year before the stock market crash and the onset of the Great Depression. Sweet Auburn's single-family homes were soon carved up into apartments, the residents transitioning to a demographic of working-class poor. King lived in what is now known as the Birth Home at 501 Auburn until he was twelve. By that time, many of Sweet Auburn's homes were in disrepair, with only 13 percent occupied by owners.[2]

Even as the residential portion of the neighborhood began to decline, the commercial side of Sweet Auburn was getting sweeter and sweeter. The business district enjoyed an extended heyday from the 1930s through the 1950s. After the Civil Rights Act passed in 1964, African Americans had more residential options as segregation slowly subsided, and Black residents and customers began to leave the neighborhood. Sweet Auburn's fortunes again dimmed, significant signs of revitalization did not emerge for more than three decades.

In 2003, with the shotgun row houses at 472-488 Auburn still in a state of disrepair, the National Park Service bought them after the tenants accepted offers to relocate following years of negotiations.

The National Park Service recognizes the critical nature of these shotgun row homes and the broader Birth Home Block for providing context about Sweet Auburn's history, especially the neighborhood's influence in shaping the mindset of the Civil Rights Movement's foremost leader. The properties remain protected and secure, but they stand vacant as historical relics rather than lived-in residences. In the future, the National Park Service could introduce them back into use via its Historic Leasing Program.

BACK WINDOWS

#1

#2

#3

#4

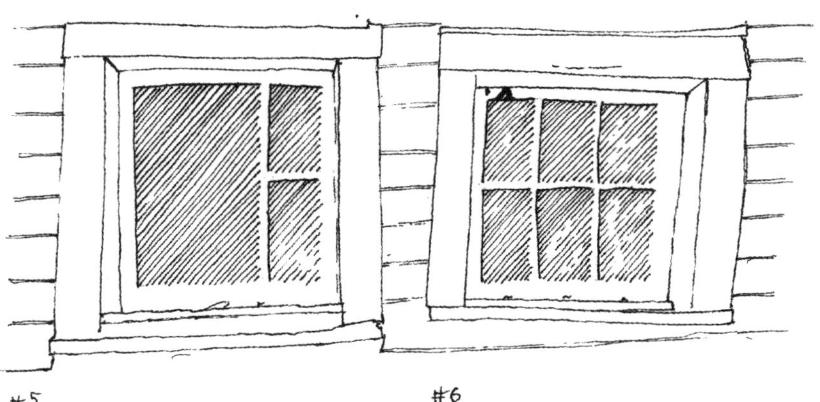

#5

#6

# Fire Station No. 6

**37-39 BOULEVARD**

The city that became Atlanta started as Terminus, a settlement of about five hundred people that took its name from its location at the endpoint of the Western & Atlantic Railroad line. It was officially incorporated in 1837 as Marthasville, named after Martha Lumpkin, the daughter of Georgia's governor, Wilson Lumpkin. The name was changed to Atlanta eleven years later—the same year the city council approved its initial volunteer fire brigade.

In November 1864, Atlanta experienced firsthand the destructive menace of fire as General William Tecumseh Sherman laid waste to the city on his March to the Sea during the Civil War. The city commissioned the professional Atlanta Fire Department in 1882 amid Reconstruction. Eight Atlanta Fire Department stations were constructed to address the increasing demand for services, and the department's protective role proved critical as the city grew into a commercial center.

Sometime shortly after noon on Monday, May 21, 1917, firefighters at Station No. 6 responded to a blaze in the neighborhood known today as the Old Fourth Ward. Wind spread the flames to four locations, stretching thin the fledgling fire department and its horse-drawn engines as they battled the blaze. The Great Fire of Atlanta went on to ravage seventy-three blocks of wooden homes, shanties, and buildings, burning for eleven hours and devastating

nearly 1.5 linear miles of the city. Some nineteen hundred properties across three hundred acres were destroyed, causing an estimated $100 million in damage in today's dollars. Some ten thousand people were displaced.

As Atlanta literally rose from the ashes, new seeds of commerce sprouted, with outdoor stalls popping up at the corner of what is now Edgewood Avenue and Jesse Hill Jr. Drive (formerly Butler Street), not far from where the fire broke out. The intersection eventually became the Sweet Auburn Curb Market, the city's oldest public market. After the fire, the city passed an ordinance banning the use of wood shingles for new construction, shaping the urban landscape. By the early 1930s, brick and stone became ubiquitous in Sweet Auburn, providing the hardy exteriors of many historic buildings still standing in the district today.

These structures include Fire Station No. 6, the oldest freestanding fire station in Atlanta and the sole commercial building on the block. Located at the corner of Boulevard and Auburn, the two-story Romanesque Revival building was designed by architecture firm Bruce & Morgan and was built from red clay bricks by Atlanta contractor Wagener & Gorenflo in 1894—a date prominently featured in terra-cotta on the front facade. Serving Sweet Auburn for the next ninety-seven years, Fire Station No. 6 embodied both form and function.

Inspirational yet simpler in design than the historic Romanesque style, the firehouse features a thoughtfully decorated front facade with an impressive arched engine bay built initially for horse-drawn hose wagons and later for motorized fire engines, while firefighters and visitors used the more human-scale street-level doorways for access. The second level continues the building's architectural style—one popular with churches and often seen on university campuses—and its affinity for arches accented by intricate, corbeled brick detailing supporting granite windowsills, arched Italianate windows, and a sense of ornamentation. As an added and aspirational touch, the lofty ambition of a blind arcade of corbeled brick arches accents the top of the wall just below the roofline.

More than just the architect's vision and talent were necessary for the construction of Fire Station No. 6: also required were an abundance of building material and brick that was readily available in Atlanta, in part via the Chattahoochee Brick Company, which was founded in 1878 on the east bank of the Chattahoochee River. In its heyday, the company generated some two hundred thousand bricks per day through the labor of convicts leased from the state, a deplorable and grievous practice akin to slavery that took advantage of human rights and capitalized on a racist system in exchange for profits.

The State of Georgia outlawed convict leasing in 1908, and the plant officially shut down the following March. According to the National Park Service's 2019 historic structure report, Fire Station

No. 6 was likely built with Chattahoochee brick, meaning that it, along with many other significant Atlanta structures, was built on the backs of wronged Black men, women, and children.

The Atlanta Fire Department did not integrate until 1963, when sixteen Black men were hired at station No. 16 on Simpson Road. The occasion should have been a civil rights milestone, but it was tinged with ongoing injustice, as the new firefighters were forced into segregated sleeping and dressing quarters. Full integration of the department came with the passage of the Civil Rights Act the following year, literally changing the face of Fire Station No. 6. Another fourteen years passed before the first women joined the department.

Fire Station No. 6 closed in 1991; four years later, it was rehabilitated and reopened, transitioning from a mission-oriented outpost to a neighborhood museum situated squarely within the Martin Luther King Jr. National Historical Park, just a few doors down from the civil rights leader's birth home. Young Martin played basketball in the lot behind the station during the 1930s. He may have seen trucks like the 1927 American LaFrance that is now on view at the museum as they left on calls. But not until he'd already spent more than a decade as a seasoned advocate for civil rights did King see Black men don the department's uniforms.

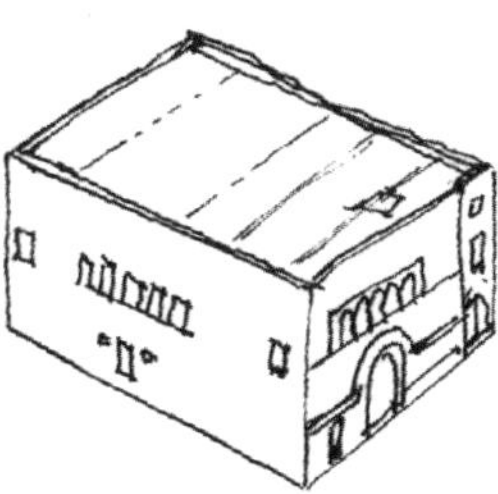

FIRE STATION NO. 6

## AN OVERVIEW

*In this chapter, we delve into the dedicated leadership of Sweet Auburn's renowned houses of worship and celebrated community organizations. We explore remarkable trailblazers and the places where they laid—and continue to lay—foundations that serve and support the neighborhood.*

*Two places integral to Sweet Auburn's legacy bookend the chapter: the King Center, a monument and memorial to Dr. King and the mission to which he gave his life, and the* SCLC*, the foremost organization of the Civil Rights Movement of the 1950s and 1960s.*

*This chapter highlights mountaintop moments but also traces captivating origin stories about spiritual homes and places of leadership that have made history. This perspective permits one truly to begin to understand just how deep the story of Sweet Auburn runs.*

CHAPTER 2

# *Leadership and Spiritual Homes*

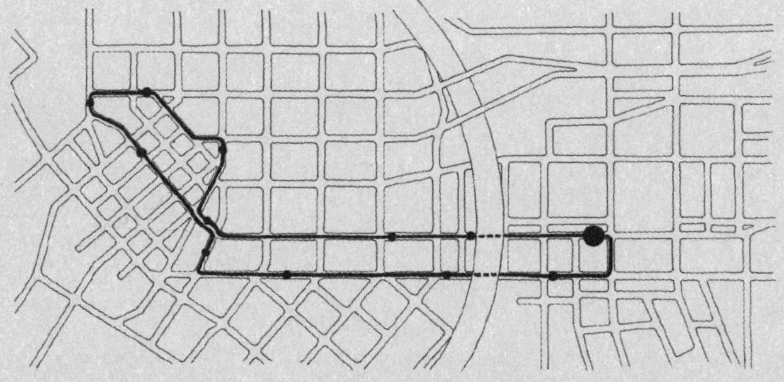

ATLANTA STREETCAR STOP: KING HISTORIC DISTRICT

**THE KING CENTER**
449 AUBURN AVENUE

**OUR LADY OF LOURDES**
25–29 BOULEVARD

**EBENEZER BAPTIST CHURCH**
407 AUBURN AVENUE

**COX BROTHERS FUNERAL HOME**
380 AUBURN AVENUE

**WHEAT STREET BAPTIST CHURCH**
359 AUBURN AVENUE

**SOUTHERN CHRISTIAN LEADERSHIP CONFERENCE (SCLC)**
330 AUBURN AVENUE

# The King Center

**449 AUBURN AVENUE**

Just weeks after her husband's assassination in 1968, Coretta Scott King found herself in the basement of their home at 234 Sunset Drive in Vine City and began to envision a living monument to commemorate his life and work. The Martin Luther King Jr. Memorial Center, as it was initially known, started with a small group of trusted advisers and family members. Coretta King served as CEO, and Christine King Farris, MLK's sister, as treasurer.

Their vision was to offer a grieving nation and unsettled world a physical place to explore the history of Dr. King's activism and understand his contributions to humanity. But in building a place to reflect on and learn from the past, they also hoped to propel his philosophy into the future, forging lasting meaning from his abrupt, senseless death.

Though the King Center was originally located at the Atlanta University Center, understanding King's work is impossible without the context Sweet Auburn provides. The neighborhood offered a young MLK Jr. a sense of security and possibility. Here, Black people were successful. Here, rich and poor came together, and support ran across class lines. Leaders mobilized for voting rights, economic and political progress, and social justice. King's neighborhood saw Atlanta's first eight Black policemen don uniforms and pose for photographs on the steps of the Butler Street YMCA. World-renowned musicians played at the Royal Peacock. Sermons rang out from pulpits. Foundations were laid, and pillars of the community

were laid to rest. For Martin Luther King Jr., this was not just a neighborhood. It was a crucible of the leadership, stewardship, and sacrifice that became the defining characteristics of his life and ultimately to embody what the King Center stands for today.

The Martin Luther King Jr. Center for Nonviolent Social Change, as it is now officially known, presents to the world King's vision of the Beloved Community, a society that rejects racism, eschews violence, embraces equality and justice, and works to eliminate poverty. Managed by the National Park Service, the center is part of the Martin Luther King Jr. National Historical Park, which also includes the Birth Home, Fire Station No. 6, the original Ebenezer Baptist Church (where King succeeded his grandfather and father as pastor and preached from 1960 until his death), and the Prince Hall Masonic Lodge (where King's operational platform, the Southern Christian Leadership Conference [SCLC], had its first office). This collection of historic sites is crucial to understanding King's life and legacy.

Today, the King Center takes an active, ongoing, and vital role in education, training, research, and scholarship. Paramount to the center's efforts is the renowned King Library and Archives, "established with a mission to promote the appropriate application of archival principles in the preservation, processing, arrangement and description of materials relevant to the life and work of Dr. Martin Luther King, Jr., and the modern civil rights movement."[1]

In addition to housing the world's most expansive collection of materials relating to Dr. King, the King Library and Archives also provides students, educators, and historians access to the foremost repository of Civil Rights Movement source material, including oral histories, records, papers, and artifacts. The King Center also features exhibitions focused on nonviolence and voter resources. However, like most things truly special, progress did not happen overnight.

> Struggle is a never-ending process. Freedom is never really won, you earn it and win it in every generation.
> —Coretta Scott King[2]

The full realization of Coretta Scott King's dream took more than a decade. During its early years, the King Center lobbied to make King's birthday, January 15, a state and federal holiday, a goal it achieved at the federal level in 1986. Construction on the King Center's current site began in 1970 with the preparation of a memorial tomb to serve as King's final resting place. His body's return from historic South-View Cemetery to Auburn Avenue in many ways represented the neighborhood's recurring role as the center of gravity in his life and movement.

In 1974, the U.S. government included the site in the newly created Martin Luther King Jr. National Historical Park, bestowing the private, nonprofit center with an additional measure of government protection. The following year, the Black-owned Atlanta Life Insurance Company, Bond Ryder James architects, and Russell Construction Company came together to design, build, and fund the King Center's administrative building. U.S. president and Georgia native Jimmy Carter, along with businessman and philanthropist Henry Ford II, raised $8 million to fund Freedom Hall, an exhibition space devoted to King's life and legacy. In 1977, the King family

opened the newly renovated Birth Home to tours, and the reflecting pool and Interfaith Chapel were completed.

With Freedom Hall's opening in 1981, construction of the King Center for Nonviolent Social Change was complete. The complex is composed of administrative offices, a museum, the King Monument, Freedom Hall, and various gathering spaces and brims with artifacts and records from King's life and the broader Civil Rights Movement. Adjacent to Freedom Hall, the tomb sits peacefully in front of an expansive reflecting pool, lovingly positioned between the center and Ebenezer. After many decades of leadership and with her husband settled, Coretta Scott King joined him there on February 7, 2006.

REV. MARTIN LUTHER KING, JR.
1929–1968
"Free at last, Free at last,
Thank God Almighty
I'm Free at last."

CORETTA SCOTT KING
1927–2006
"And now abide Faith, Hope,
Love, These Three; but the
Greatest of these is Love."
1 Cor. 13:13

# Our Lady of Lourdes

**25-29 BOULEVARD**

In 1911, Father Ignatius Lissner, a French-born Roman Catholic priest representing the Society of African Missions, began to search for a site for Atlanta's first Catholic mission dedicated to serving Blacks and Native Americans. What he found in the region was pervasive animosity toward Catholics and Blacks alike.

With perseverance and financial assistance from Catholic luminaries, Lissner purchased a plot of land on what is now Boulevard, just south of Auburn, in March 1912. Just eight months later, construction of the Our Lady of Lourdes Colored Mission was finished, and the three-story building was blessed and dedicated. In between the first-floor sanctuary and the third-floor parish hall were classrooms for the newly inaugurated Our Lady of Lourdes Catholic School, which operated until funding dried up nearly ninety years later.

The ministry's original financial support came from Mother Katharine Drexel (later Saint Katharine Drexel), a Philadelphia heiress and founder of the Sisters of the Blessed Sacrament, an order of nuns expressly organized to serve Black and Indian people.

Drexel and Lissner envisioned Our Lady of Lourdes as a memorial to the late archbishop Patrick Ryan, also of Philadelphia, who had overseen the erection of 170 churches and 82 schools during his twenty-seven-year tenure. In addition, he had founded two Black congregations and had served on the U.S. Indian Commission under President Theodore Roosevelt. In 1911, Ryan died on February 11,

the feast day of Our Lady of Lourdes, which commemorates the day in 1858, when Saint Bernadette saw the first of eighteen reputed apparitions of the Blessed Virgin Mary in a grotto near her home in Lourdes, France. The site is now one of the holiest in Roman Catholicism, and pilgrims flock from all over the world to visit the grotto, shrine, and cathedral and to drink and bathe in the water.

Today, the Sweet Auburn mission's original building, a brick structure ensconced within stone walls, still sits at 29 Boulevard. Now known as the Katharine Drexel Community Center, it houses church offices, religious education classrooms, a rehearsal hall, and the Drexel Institute for the Arts. A single-story sanctuary building was added in 1960 at 25 Boulevard, and worshippers still gather there for Sunday Mass.

In addition to hearing a good sermon at Our Lady of Lourdes, parishioners—and partiers—can visit Sister Louisa's Church of the

Living Room & Ping Pong Emporium just across the street at the corner of Boulevard and Edgewood. The church-themed bar features karaoke with an organ and, as the name indicates, weekly Ping-Pong tournaments. Other hot spots on the block include Biggerstaff Brewing Company and local favorite coffee shop Chrome Yellow Trading Co. A few blocks east, the Thumbs Up Diner offers a hearty breakfast menu and friendly staff.

Eat. Pray. Ping-Pong—all in Sweet Auburn.

# Ebenezer Baptist Church

**407 AUBURN AVENUE**

*Ebenezer* comes from the Hebrew word meaning "stone of help." The church carrying this name has been a rock of the Sweet Auburn community since its founding in 1886. Known worldwide for its famous pastors Martin Luther King Sr. ("Daddy King"); his son, Martin Luther King Jr.; and U.S. senator Raphael Warnock, who has been the church's senior pastor since 2005, Ebenezer Baptist Church is both an active place of worship and the spiritual home of the Civil Rights Movement. Ebenezer is central not only to the Martin Luther King Jr. National Historical Park but to understanding his life and times.

The church began with a handful of congregants led by the Reverend John A. Parker from 1886 to 1894 at a site on Airline Street but had grown to well over four hundred parishioners by the time land was acquired in 1914 under the leadership of Parker's successor, the Reverend Adam Daniel Williams, King's maternal grandfather. Day laborers then began constructing the new sanctuary at the corner of Auburn Avenue and Jackson Street, with members worshiping in the roofed basement while the rest of the structure was built out around them. Gothic in style, the church cost $40,000

EBENEZER BAPTIST

to build and was completed in 1922. The building permit shows no architect of record.

Williams not only oversaw the physical building of the church but also laid the spiritual foundation necessary for the ascent of Sweet Auburn and for the empowerment of his people. Although Williams had been born into slavery in 1861, he chose to celebrate January 2, 1863, as his birthday—the day after President Abraham Lincoln issued the Emancipation Proclamation, which provided that persons enslaved in the states that had rebelled against the Union "are, and henceforward shall be free." That group included A. D. Williams's father, also a preacher.

A founding member of the Atlanta chapter of the NAACP, and a sermonizer from the start, Williams lived, breathed, and preached about equal opportunity in both the spiritual and material realms. His grandson later adopted these beliefs and shared them with the world as what King described as an "advocator of the social gospel," a system and framework of equality concerned "with the whole man, not only his soul but his body, not only his spiritual well-being, but his material well-being."[1]

Listed on the National Register of Historic Places, Ebenezer consistently contributed to King's community engagement and spiritual development. Daddy King was serving as assistant pastor there when his older son was born, and young Martin was ordained there at age nineteen and became co-pastor in 1960.

The pulpit offered Dr. King a platform not only from which to teach spiritual lessons but also where he could hone the oratorical skills that would give voice to the fight for equality and to the moral ethic behind the strategy of nonviolent resistance. Ebenezer was a constant source of social refuge and spiritual replenishment for the duration of his life.

The day after King's April 4, 1968, assassination in Memphis, Tennessee, a funeral service was held at the city's R. S. Lewis Funeral Home. On April 9, family and friends held a second memorial at Ebenezer that was followed by a somber procession to King's alma mater, Morehouse College, and a final public farewell ceremony there. An estimated one hundred thousand mourners accompanied the slain leader's casket as it made the journey of more than three miles on a mule-drawn wagon. Morehouse president Benjamin Mays, a legendary educator whom King had called "my spiritual mentor and my intellectual father," gave the eulogy, fulfilling their mutual promise that whichever man survived longer would offer a homily at the other's funeral.[2] Mays described the experience as akin to "eulogiz[ing] his deceased son."[3]

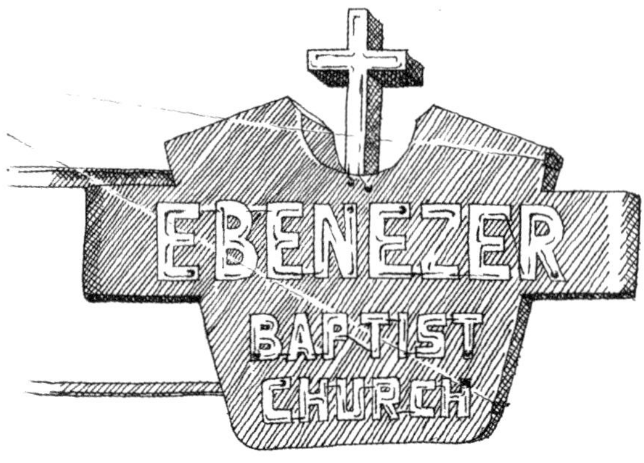


The King family again mourned at Ebenezer in 1974 when a gunman fatally wounded Dr. King's mother there as she played the organ during the Lord's Prayer "less than 100 yards from where her famous son . . . is buried."[4]

Each January, Martin Luther King Jr. Day brings large crowds to the church's modern home, built across the street from the Heritage Sanctuary in 1999. Situated in the National Historical Park, the church's newer Horizon Sanctuary has drawn famous speakers, including U.S. presidents, civil rights icons, and politicians on both the local and national levels.

More recently, Ebenezer has returned to its roots as a wellspring of political activism: in 2020, Raphael Warnock, the church's fifth senior pastor, won election as Georgia's first Black U.S. senator. Warnock has said that as he represents the state in the nation's highest legislative body, he strives to embody the values of the Beloved Community, a concept popularized by King during his leadership of the Civil Rights Movement.

# Cox Brothers Funeral Home

**380 AUBURN AVENUE**

In the Jim Crow–era South, Black people had little control over the outside world, suffering from a parade of indignities in a racist system. At home in tight-knit communities, however, they had each other. They had businesses and services as well as churches, where they could look beyond earthly suffering and envision the eternal freedom and joy that lay ahead in the world beyond. Churches offered hope.

Death and burial rituals provided moments of autonomy for a community whose pain was largely ignored by its oppressors. Homegoing ceremonies provided a rare opportunity to cultivate and follow Black customs without white interference.

In the days of slavery, Blacks were relegated largely to unmarked graves hidden away in forgotten corners of massive plantations. In rare cases, the graves received rudimentary markers, most of which have been lost to time.

As Black people gained agency during Reconstruction, they sought to provide members of their communities with dignity in death and soon established Black-owned funeral homes. One of Sweet Auburn's earliest Black businesses was Cox Brothers Funeral Directors, established in 1900 by Emily S. Cox and her sons, Charles and Allen, at 69 South Pryor Street. The company constructed a building at 258 Auburn Avenue in 1923 and operated there for

COX BROTHERS FUNERAL HOME
380 AUBURN AVE NE
COX
BROS
Cigars
OPEN

another dozen years, working together with florists, transportation services, and cemeteries to bring comfort to the community.

In 1940, the company altered its name to Cox Brothers Funeral Home and moved to a building at 380 Auburn Avenue that had been constructed eleven years earlier to serve as a restaurant and a market. Added later was the structure's trademark front facade, with gold latticework featuring repeating cubes running in a linear fashion. Cox Brothers remained at this historic address until it closed in 2019, starting many prominent figures off on their final journeys. According to the National Park Service, Cox Brothers offered Atlanta's first motorized hearse, and one of its frequent destinations was Oakland Cemetery, just a mile away in Grant Park. The city purchased the first six acres of what was originally called Atlanta Cemetery in 1850, and it subsequently became the final resting place for thousands of Black people. In keeping with the community's burial traditions, graves were marked with wood, flowers, and shrubs, and their loss over the ensuing century and a half has resulted in an estimated 872 unmarked graves at Oakland. Many originated in a section known as Slave Square—segregated grounds mandated by an 1852 Atlanta City Council ruling that Blacks and whites were to be buried separately. In 1877, these bodies were exhumed and moved to a section dubbed the colored pauper grounds, a sprawling, unplanned memorial providing a message from the past and a lesson for the future. As Dr. D. L. Henderson has noted, the configuration of the cemetery is an unfortunate reminder of a society with misplaced values:

> While cemeteries are cultural repositories of local history and the values and beliefs of the people who use them, they're also microcosms of society. And, you can look at the time period in which they developed and see

the values and beliefs of the people, and part of those values and beliefs were that a segregated society was the way things should be.[1]

Many notable Black Atlantans are memorialized in what became known as the African American Grounds with headstones and

markers that contribute to Oakland's exceptional beauty and historic value. Among others, these include:

**Selena Sloan Butler:** One of the first graduates of Spelman Seminary (now Spelman College) and founder of the first parent-teacher association for African American children in the United States (Block 68, Lot 6, Grave 6).

**Bishop Wesley John Gaines:** Second pastor at Big Bethel AME, a formerly enslaved person, and founder of Morris Brown College (Block 65, Lot 1, Grave 2).

**Carrie Steele Logan:** A freedwoman who established the Carrie Steele-Pitts Home, Atlanta's first African American orphanage (Block 64, Lot 5).

In addition, Maynard Jackson Jr., Atlanta's first Black mayor (1938–2003) is buried at the northwest corner of the North Public Grounds.[2]

Not until 1886, with the founding of South-View Cemetery, did Black families have a cemetery to call their own. South-View lies on one hundred acres of gentle hills southeast of Sweet Auburn in Lakewood Heights. South-View offers a scenic glimpse of Victorian-era funerary art and a sense of reverence for the more than eighty thousand African Americans who rest there.

Nine Black businessmen founded South-View to combat the racial oppression that followed Atlanta's Black residents even to the grave. The founders envisioned a place that differed from Oakland and other places of burial in terms of both landscape architecture and employment of Black burial rites. The State of Georgia granted the cemetery's charter in April 1886, two months after the founders laid out their initial vision.

Those who rest at South-View include some of Atlanta's most influential figures, among them twenty-two people for whom public schools have been named and all of Ebenezer Baptist Church's deceased pastors. Dr. Martin Luther King Jr. was first interred at South-View in 1968 before being reinterred at the King Center for Nonviolent Social Change, where his widow, Coretta Scott King, joined him at her death. King's immediate family, including his parents and brother, A. D. Williams King, are buried at South-View. King's spiritual father, Dr. Benjamin Mays, who served as president of Morehouse College from 1940 to 1967, was initially buried at South-View, although he and his wife, Sadie Gray Mays, were moved to a gravesite at the college in 1995. Mays's eulogy of King, "No Man Is Ahead of His Time," has been called "a masterpiece of twentieth century oratory" and will forever connect the two men.[3]

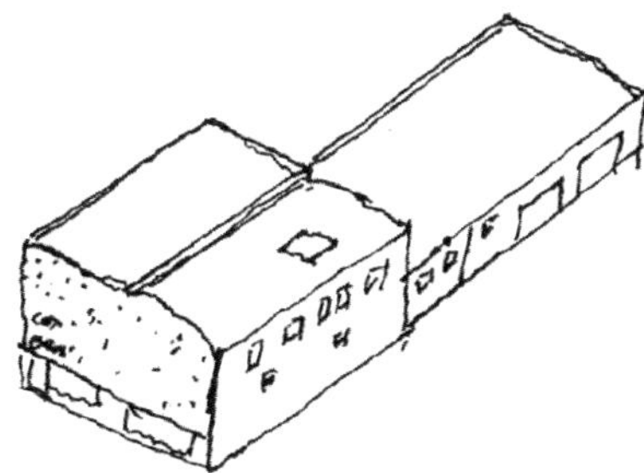

South-View also serves as the final resting place for prominent Atlantans Hank Aaron, Moses Amos, Julian Bond, the Reverend William Holmes Borders, Ariel Serena Hedges Bowen, “Mama” Carrie Cunningham, Charles Lincoln Harper, Alonzo Herndon, Jesse Hill Jr., U.S. Representative John Lewis, and Herman J. Russell as well as two Tuskegee Airmen. Sweet Auburn forefather John Wesley Dobbs and his wife, Irene Thompson Dobbs, are buried there, along with three of their six daughters: Dr. Irene Dobbs Jackson, Millicent Dobbs Jordan, and Mattiwilda Dobbs Janzon.

Today, South-View's president, Winifred Watts Hemphill, great-granddaughter of the cemetery's cofounder and first treasurer, Albert Watts, carries on a family tradition of respect, dignity, and grace. In 2004, the grounds and their legacy were protected by the formation of the Historic South-View Preservation Foundation, which took as its “mission to record, interpret, restore and preserve the art, history and environment of Historic South-View.”[4]

This ethos of preservation has been embraced only relatively recently as part of an effort to rectify the historical assault on Black memory. The Sweet Auburn neighborhood's 1976 designation as a National Historic Landmark District constituted the first step on the road to protecting these sacred spaces, preserving churches and funeral homes within its nineteen-acre boundary.

These efforts bring hope for further change. In December 2022, Congress created the African American Burial Grounds Preservation Program, providing important protection for Black cemeteries and helping to ensure the sanctity of these hallowed grounds.

As Dr. Kami Fletcher, associate professor of American and African American History at Albright College, notes, such efforts to preserve African American burial sites constitute the latest example of the resiliency that has always characterized the Black experience in America: "Every tradition Black folks practice today is born out of a period of enslavement that tried to crush our humanity and erase our African roots. But it was through death that we lived!"[5]

# Wheat Street Baptist Church

**359 AUBURN AVENUE**

In 1869, members of West Atlanta's First Baptist Church (now Friendship Baptist Church) who lived across town sought to create a place of worship closer to their homes. With the blessing of First Baptist's founding pastor, Frank Quarles, they found a site in Sweet Auburn and launched Mount Pleasant Baptist. The congregation initially met in the Reverend Andrew Jackson's yard on Howell Street under a bush arbor, planting spiritual roots in what became a pivotal community. With strong leaders and generations of solid stewardship, the surrounding land and the church itself proved fertile ground for innovations designed to cultivate Black wealth and activism.

Six years after its founding, the congregation named its first official pastor, William Henry Tillman, who saw membership swell to one thousand during his twenty-two-year tenure and positioned the church for further growth. In the 1880s, Mount Pleasant found a permanent home at the intersection of Fort and Old Wheat Streets (now Auburn Avenue), and the church's renamed itself Wheat Street Baptist Church. Today, that name is synonymous with success and prestige.

Like many late nineteenth-century African American churches, Wheat Street provided space and support to help community organizations flourish. Among the most celebrated is the Butler

Street Young Men's Christian Association (YMCA), which was formed in the basement of the church building by J. S. Brandon in 1894. By that time, though, Wheat Street already had a long history as a staging ground for empowerment and economic activism.

In July 1881, five hundred washerwomen met in the church to plan a strike for better pay and greater autonomy. The meeting resulted in the formation of the Washing Society, whose membership ballooned to more than three thousand within three weeks. The timing was excellent, with the strikers gaining leverage from the fact that the effort began less than a month before the International Cotton Exposition, which sought to stress that Blacks and whites could work together in commerce. Originally convinced that the strike would fail, the *Atlanta Constitution* reluctantly praised the fortitude of the walkout participants as they persevered through fines, arrests, and other attempts at intimidation. Atlanta mayor James W. English—historically infamous for his exploitation and abuse of convict laborers at the Chattahoochee Brick Company—eventually approved moderate concessions to the strikers' demands, including a wage increase averaging between four and eight dollars per month. Perhaps more important, the strike—and the church—put an early spotlight on Black labor and its contributions to the city's functioning, a tactic that future civil rights leaders also employed.

In 1897, Tillman stepped down for health reasons. After a year of interim leadership, the Reverend Peter James Bryant stepped into the pulpit, guiding the congregation through a period of exponential growth: over the next two decades, Wheat Street added more than three thousand new members.

Complementing his position and place in the pulpit, Bryant spoke to the community through the *Voice of The Negro*, a white-owned but

Black-edited newspaper where he served as associate editor. The *Voice of The Negro* helped magnify the accomplishments of Black Atlantans both within the community and among white readers. By all accounts a brilliant thinker, Bryant also created the Atlanta Benevolent and Protective Association in the early 1900s to care for church members and nonmembers in need. In 1905, Bryant sold the association to former enslaved person and legendary entrepreneur Alonzo Herndon, who folded it into his Atlanta Life Insurance Company.

With progress, however, also came setbacks. The Great Fire of 1917 destroyed Wheat Street's original building, along with more than nineteen hundred other homes and buildings in Old Fourth Ward. Under Bryant's leadership, a new Gothic Revival–style building was constructed at the corner of Auburn and Yonge Street (William Holmes Borders Sr. Drive). The church includes twenty-two departmental offices and classrooms, a twenty-five-hundred-seat

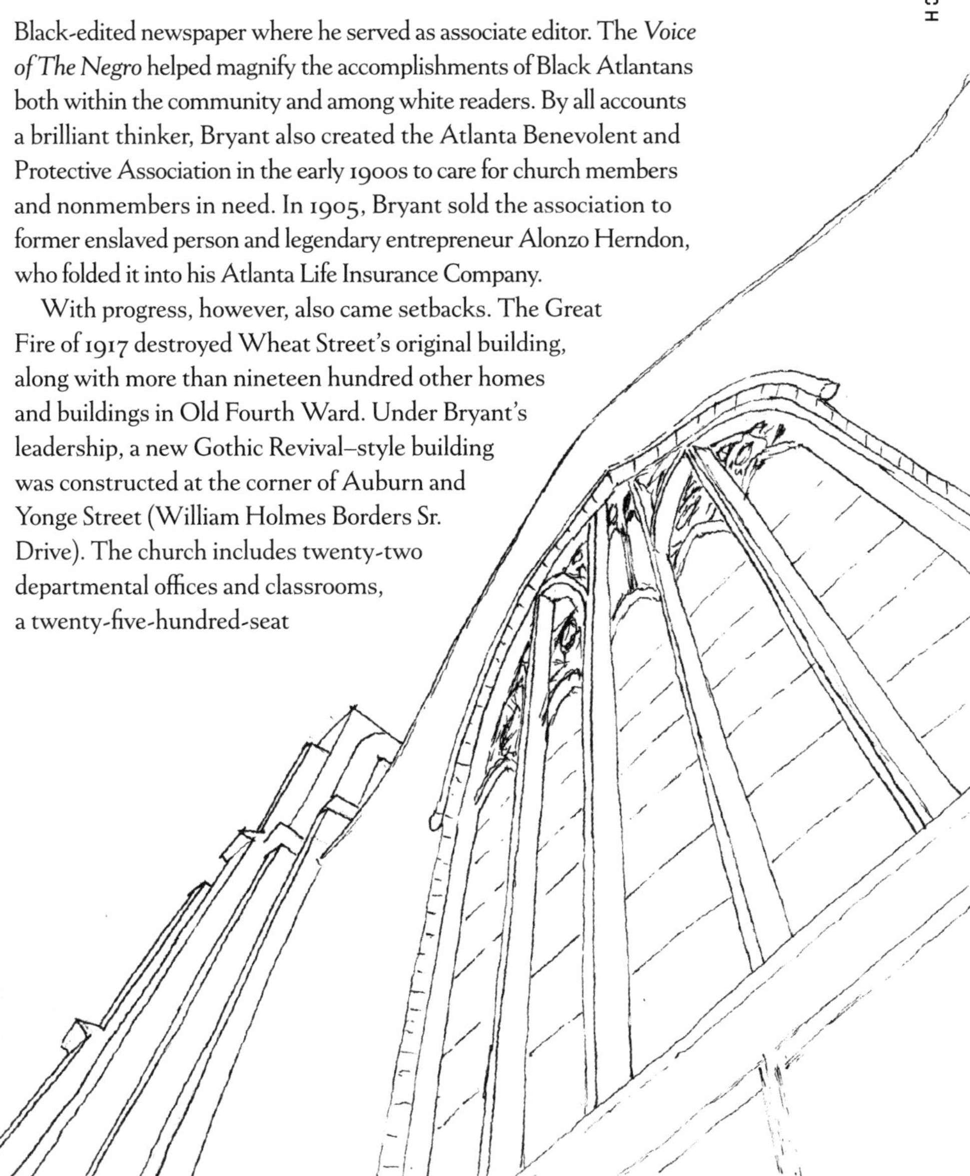

sanctuary, and an inspiring vaulted ceiling. The Christian Education Building, clad in a similarly classic stone exterior, was added in 1955.

With Rev. Bryant's passing in 1929 and the ensuing devastation of the Great Depression, the church suffered severe financial setbacks. In 1930, the Reverend J. Raymond Henderson began a seven-year term at the helm, but it was marked by turmoil over the church's debt. Henderson gave way to Wheat Street's longest-serving and perhaps most distinguished pastor, the Reverend William Holmes Borders Sr., who served until 1985. A civil rights leader, teacher, and humanitarian, the ever-progressive Borders helped to reinforce Wheat Street as a cornerstone of the power structure of Sweet Auburn and the Civil Rights Movement with bold preaching and real estate prowess.

In addition to completing the present-day structure, Borders arranged the church's purchase of thirty-two acres of land in the neighborhood with the goal of benefiting the broader community. The buildings erected under his leadership not only facilitated spiritual education but pioneered affordable housing with projects that included the Wheat Street Gardens apartment complex and the Wheat Street Towers, a 1973 high-rise that was the first church-backed senior living facility to receive federal housing subsidies. While the Gardens complex later fell into disrepair and was demolished, the Towers underwent a $24 million renovation in 2019 that improved the facade as well as added amenities including a skyline lounge with views of the city and a collection of African American memorabilia. During the 1950s, Rev. Borders and Wheat Street Baptist also introduced the first church-run credit union, a modern take on the ethos of mutual assistance that the church had helped bring into existence.

Borders's financial aptitude was complemented by innovations in evangelistic communication that fixed his position in the city across racial lines. He started a weekly radio show, *Seven Minutes at the Mike*, where he spread the Gospel through impeccably composed sermons received far beyond the confines of the segregated neighborhood where he preached. The broadcasts influenced a young Martin Luther King Jr., among many others.

WHEAT STREET BAPTIST

King was also influenced by Borders's wife, Julia Pate Borders, who served as the boy's English

teacher. The first lady of Wheat Street served for twenty-seven years as Wheat Street's unpaid director of Christian education, helping run the Sunday School, Vacation Bible School, Head Start, nursery, and other programs.

After offering a lifetime of service to Wheat Street Baptist Church, Atlanta, the United States, and the world, Rev. Borders became pastor emeritus in 1989. Four years later, he was laid to rest and buried alongside his wife at South-View Cemetery.

Since 1875, Wheat Street Baptist Church has only had six permanent pastors:

William Henry Tillman (1875–97)
Peter James Bryant (1898–1929)
J. Raymond Henderson (1939–37)
William Holmes Borders Sr. (1937–89)
Dr. Michael Neely Harris (1989–2015)
Dr. Ralph Basui Watkins (2017–20)

Wheat Street has had an interim pastor since Dr. Watkins's departure.

# Southern Christian Leadership Conference (SCLC)

**PRINCE HALL MASONIC LODGE**
**330 AUBURN AVENUE**

That a movement can be advanced by sitting still is perhaps a fitting metaphor for the Black struggle for equality in the United States, where a dramatic fight was won by men, women, and children with enough internal fortitude to eschew violence and perfect the strategy of the sit-in.

In early December 1955 in Montgomery, Alabama, Rosa Parks, a seasoned activist, famously refused to give up her seat in the "colored" section of a bus to a white passenger. Four days later, Parks's simple act of defiance was followed by the Montgomery Bus Boycott, a groundswell of indignant civil disobedience carried out in large part by women. This action inspired the broader Civil Rights Movement and carried clear ramifications for Sweet Auburn, more than 150 miles away in neighboring Georgia.

Parks's seminal contributions to American life garnered perhaps their most notable recognition when President Bill Clinton awarded her the Presidential Medal of Freedom in 1996 and when she received the Congressional Gold Medal three years later. At her death in 2005, she became the first woman to lie in honor in the U.S. Capitol's rotunda.

The strategic lessons learned from the arrest of the Mother of the Freedom Movement helped spur on the cause in her day and long after. A lawsuit filed on behalf of other women mistreated during the boycott used the Equal Protection Clause of the Fourteenth Amendment to argue that the segregation of the local bus system was unconstitutional. The U.S. Supreme Court accepted that argument, ruling on December 21, 1956, in *Browder v. Gayle* that public transportation systems could not discriminate.

Centuries after enslaved people organized their first consequential revolts and more than a decade after Black soldiers returned from World War II and faced the cruel irony that a country could ask them to die for rights unsecured for themselves, the modern Civil Rights Movement began to crystallize. The *Browder* case showed the effectiveness of a two-pronged approach that combined nonviolent mass action with legal action designed to change the political landscape.

Over the next few decades, movement leaders followed this strategy, which they formalized during a caucus at Atlanta's Morehouse College that brought together Martin Luther King Jr. and fellow up-and-coming civil rights leaders Ralph David Abernathy, Bayard Rustin, Charles Kenzie Steele, Fred Shuttlesworth, and Joseph E. Lowery. On January 10–11, 1957, these men gathered with more than fifty other Black ministers and community leaders at Ebenezer Baptist Church and founded the Southern Leadership Conference on Transportation and Nonviolent Integration, which would pursue the twin strategies of nonviolence and litigation. These leaders believed "that civil rights are essential to democracy, that segregation must end, and that all Black people should reject segregation absolutely and nonviolently."[1]

Three weeks later, members of the nascent organization gathered in New Orleans to elect leaders. Known for his oratory and courageous actions, King was a natural fit as the organization's spokesperson and first president. The group then held its first convention on August 8, 1957, in Montgomery, officially adopting the name Southern Christian Leadership Conference (SCLC).

From its inception, the organization focused on working in the South and aligning with local direct-action groups; the inclusion of *Christian* in the organization's name highlighted the importance of rooting it in the church. These decisions set the tone and ethos and narrowed down options for headquarters. Atlanta proved the perfect choice: the African American community in King's hometown had strong leaders and a substantial middle class, numerous historically Black colleges, and an extensive network of churches.

King moved the SCLC into a small office at the Prince Hall Masonic Lodge at 330 Auburn Avenue, a handsome three-story yellow- and red-brick building stacked high with a long and distinguished history. Nearly all of the initial staffers were female. The first full-time hire was Ella Josephine Baker, who had already had a long career as an organizer, mentor, and champion of equality. Baker admired and emulated Parks, becoming a driving force for an organization where men took center stage and women's significant contributions went largely unrecognized.

Born on December 13, 1903, in Virginia, Baker grew up in a tight-knit family of modest means, hearing her grandmother's stories of slavery and developing an unbeatable spirit and strong sense of social justice. Although Baker often declared, "Strong people don't need strong leaders," she nevertheless inspired many students from across the nation to assert their individual wills in service of collective impact.[2]

A grassroots organizer at heart, Baker studied at Shaw University in Raleigh, North Carolina, becoming valedictorian despite

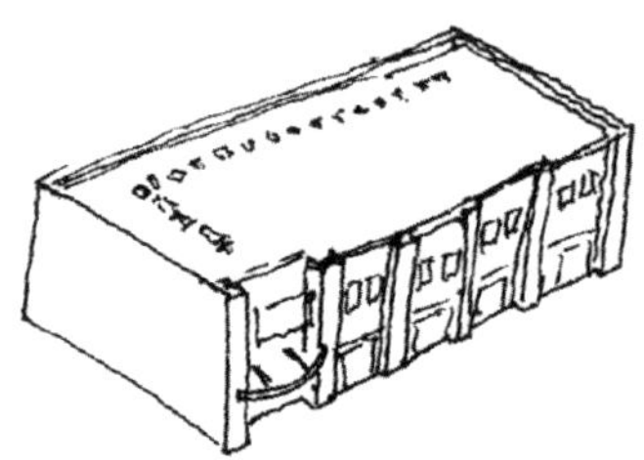

SCLC NATIONAL OFFICE

questioning the school's dress code and leaders' racial attitudes. In the 1940s, Baker became the highest-ranking woman at the NAACP, building friendships with those sharing common interests and communal concern. Inspired by Parks's activism in 1955, Baker cofounded a Jim Crow resistance group, In Friendship, before joining forces with King and others at the SCLC and ultimately becoming the group's executive secretary, a role that testified both to her power as an organizer and to the sexism that kept her from true leadership positions.

While working with the SCLC, Baker also led Crusade for Citizenship, an organization promoting voter registration. She relished direct action and ultimately departed the SCLC to help student activists develop faith in themselves. Bent on empowering younger generations, she insisted that students should create their own organization, and the Student Nonviolent Coordinating Committee (SNCC) was born just up the street from 330 Auburn Avenue.

Baker's success was symbiotic, requiring others to believe in her as much as she believed in them. Determined, untiring, and always giving of herself, she defined the movement but did not shy away from criticizing its gender discrimination and other shortcomings. At her death on December 13, 1986, her goal of seeing women recognized for their labors was not yet fully realized.

Baker's contributions to the SCLC helped the organization attain national attention and influence. Under King's leadership, groups that Baker and others supported—the SCLC, SNCC, and the Congress of Racial Equality (CORE)—worked together on collective actions that resounded across the United States. SNCC spearheaded the 1961 Freedom Rides, while the SCLC organized the 1963 March on Washington and the Selma-to-Montgomery March two years later.

While these landmark moments were achieved in unity, fostering togetherness was not simply a formality. It took intentional work. Black churches feared allowing religion to be used as a political tool, and elder statesmen in the Black community, including Martin Luther King Sr., argued that records of arrest for protesting could later be used against young people. Even as elders were wary of what they viewed as SCLC's aggressive tactics, some groups pushed for even more confrontational measures.

The March on Washington constituted a compromise between these viewpoints, blending peaceful engagement with powerful messaging and mass mobilization. On July 2, 1963, Martin Luther King Jr., along with A. Philip Randolph and Bayard Rustin (who as a gay man was later forced into a less visible role in the movement), met with SNCC's John Lewis and James Farmer Jr. of CORE to plan the march in the nation's capital to display a united front against segregation.

Fear flowed through Washington, D.C., as worst-case scenarios played out in the minds of political leaders and in the press. However, some three hundred thousand protesters converged on the city on August 28 with no violence or riots, signaling to the world that the achievement of civil rights was—more clearly than ever before—within reach. Those in attendance heard King's earth-shaking "I Have a Dream" speech.

Back in the Deep South, however, almost two more years of violent resistance passed before the movement got closer to the promised land. With the guarantees of the Civil Rights Act of 1964 unrealized, the Selma Voting Rights Campaign was launched to dismantle discriminatory voting practices. On March 7, 1965, approximately six hundred protesters led by SNCC's Lewis and the SCLC's Hosea Williams marched across the Edmund Pettus Bridge in Selma, Alabama, toward one of the most disturbing moments in U.S. history.

An internationally televised tragedy, "Bloody Sunday" brought bullwhips, tear gas and billy clubs from the hands of Alabama law enforcement into the homes of a traumatized country. As King had predicted, citizens across the land were appalled by the brutality of the crackdown and let their voices be heard. President Lyndon Johnson quickly convened a joint session of Congress and just eight days after the march urged passage of a voting reform bill. The Voting Rights Act became law on August 6, and Johnson labeled Selma "a turning point in man's unending search for freedom."[3]

The SCLC was a vital contributor to this history. After King's assassination, the group left 330 Auburn for the building two doors down, the Charles R. Steele Jr. building at 320 Auburn. Sandwiched between these two homes of the SCLC is the vertically oriented Tabor Building at 328 Auburn, a three-story brick structure with its own history of civic engagement. Built in 1927 as a home for the International Order of Twelve Knights and Daughters of Tabor, which started as an antislavery society, the Tabor name was associated with philanthropic hospitals the society built around the

United States. In 1995, the building was purchased and renovated for office space by the SCLC Women's Organizational Movement for Equality Now (WOMEN), founded by Evelyn Lowery, wife of Joseph Lowery.

Two years after Evelyn Lowery's 2013 death, a civic arts group, the Loss Prevention, dedicated the Evelyn Lowery "HERO" mural at the corner of Auburn Avenue and Bell Street. The artwork (now painted over) not only recognized Lowery's contributions to the cause but also illuminated the importance of the struggle for equality.

The SCLC's original home, the Prince Hall Masonic Lodge of Georgia, also witnessed its fair share of struggle long before the organization started making civil rights history there. Designed in 1937, the structure presented extraordinary challenges for the masons and for John Wesley Dobbs, the lodge's grand master from 1932 onward, who sought to have the project serve as the cornerstone of his career.

A mason's cornerstone not only is literally important for a physical edifice but also symbolizes persistence in the pursuit of sturdiness, morality, and truth. The hollowed-out cornerstone of the Prince Hall Masonic Lodge testifies to Dobbs's devotion and strife, holding a Bible, placed there by his fifth daughter, Mattiwilda. Lovingly hidden inside the holy book by her younger sister, June Dobbs Butts, is a four-leaf clover, there to bring good luck and to acknowledge her father's trials and accomplishments in realizing his dream of seeing the building rise. Construction was completed in 1941.

The facade features the most widely recognized symbols of Freemasonry, the Square and Compasses. In 1955, celebrated Black architect Edward C. Miller designed an addition, expanding the building's tradition of supporting Black commerce and civic calling. Joining the Masons under one roof was WERD, the first Black-owned radio station in the United States and a powerful outlet through which King shared his message and mission. Also located in the building were offices of the Atlanta Civic-Political League and the Brotherhood of Sleeping Car Porters as well as the Madame C. J. Walker Beauty Shoppe, part of a sprawling enterprise that enabled Walker to become the country's first Black female self-made millionaire. The first floor housed offices for MLK and staff, with additional offices, a printing press, and a photography darkroom located in the basement.

Thanks to the work of one notable Prince Hall Mason, SNCC activist turned member of the U.S. Congress John Lewis, 330 Auburn Avenue was added to the Martin Luther King Jr. National Historical Park in 2018, setting in motion a plan to restore and preserve the landmark building.

The Masons and their female counterparts, the Eastern Stars, will continue to occupy the building. As a consequence of efforts by longtime Masons Edward Bowen and Edward Driver, with help from architectural firm Lord, Aeck & Sargent and preservation lead Karen Gravel, the building is currently undergoing extensive renovations that will turn it into a sixteen-thousand-square-foot multiuse space highlighting the remarkable women and men who worked side-by-side to build up a community and make history.

PRINCE HALL GRAND LODGE
330 AUBURN AVE NE
AUBURN AVE

## AN OVERVIEW

*John Wesley Dobbs, the unofficial mayor of Sweet Auburn during its heyday, used "Bucks, Ballots, and Books" as both a slogan and a philosophy. He believed that members of his community could travel down the path toward freedom by engaging in commerce, registering to vote, and pursuing education. Dobbs's leadership helped bring that destination into view.*

*As a Mason, Dobbs not only knew how to build but understood that building well requires planning and precise execution. The sights found in this chapter commemorate mutual progress that relied on the action-oriented support of local, national, and in some cases international stakeholders.*

*One of the fun things about this chapter is the diversity in how Sweet Auburn legends were made. The chapter showcases radio stations and Odd Fellows, entrepreneurship and ghosts of the past, works of art and the art of politics, and ultimately "Black City Hall."*

CHAPTER 3

# DOBBS

*Bucks, Ballots, and Books*

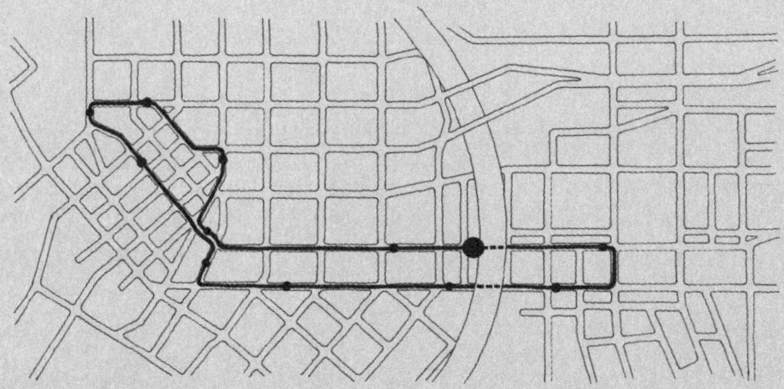

ATLANTA STREETCAR STOP: DOBBS PLAZA

**THE PRINCE HALL MASONIC LODGE**
330 AUBURN AVENUE

**JOHN WESLEY DOBBS PLAZA**
AUBURN AVENUE AT FORT STREET

**ODD FELLOWS BUILDING AND ANNEX**
228–250 AUBURN AVENUE

**GOLD DUST TWINS AND THE ATLANTA LIFE LOCAL BRANCH**
229–243 AUBURN AVENUE

**BIG BETHEL AFRICAN METHODIST EPISCOPAL (AME) CHURCH**
220 AUBURN AVENUE

**JOHN LEWIS HERO MURAL**
SOUTHWEST CORNER OF AUBURN AVENUE AND JESSE HILL JR. DRIVE

**BUTLER STREET YMCA**
22 JESSE HILL JR. DRIVE

# The Prince Hall Masonic Lodge

**SOUTHERN CHRISTIAN LEADERSHIP CONFERENCE (SCLC)**
**WERD RADIO STATION**
**330 AUBURN AVENUE**

A beautiful historic building, the Prince Hall Masonic Lodge honors a man and the movement he spurred. Born enslaved in Barbados sometime between 1735 and 1738, Prince Hall was moved to Massachusetts by his enslaver, William Hall, in 1765. Freed five years later, Prince Hall obtained an education, purchased a home, voted, and paid taxes, becoming a champion of equality. Prior to his death in 1807, he devoted himself to providing educational access for Black children.

Hall worked within Boston's free Black community for the abolitionist cause and is considered the founder of Black Freemasonry in the United States, which is today known as Prince Hall Freemasonry. His moving 1797 speech to the African Lodge in Cambridge, Massachusetts, demonstrated his talent for writing and public speaking, positioning revolts by enslaved Haitians and others as sources of hope for Black Americans' struggle for equality:

> My brethren, let us not be cast down under these and many other abuses we at present are laboring under—for the darkest hour is just before the break of day. My brethren, let us remember what a dark day it was with our African brethren, six years ago, in the French West Indies. Nothing but the snap of the whip was heard, from morning to evening. Hanging, breaking on the wheel, burning, and all manner of tortures, were inflicted on those unhappy people. But, blessed be God, the scene is changed.[1]

Like its namesake, Sweet Auburn's Prince Hall Masonic Lodge stands with distinction. It is "Square, Plumb and Level" (a mantra of the Masons), fundamental attributes of a physical and spiritual structure built to last. The building was designed by architects Charles Hopson and Ross Howard in the Renaissance Revival style. John Wesley Dobbs, the unofficial mayor of Sweet Auburn and grand master of the lodge from 1932 to 1961, led the fundraising and development effort. Construction took place between 1937 and 1941. As a tribute to Dobbs's hard work and fortitude, two of his daughters, June Dobbs Butts and Mattiwilda Dobbs, laid a Bible with a four-leaf clover pressed between its pages behind the cornerstone. A 1955 renovation brought an addition designed by Edward C. Miller, a well-regarded Black architect.

Within a year after the 1957 founding of the Southern Christian Leadership Conference (SCLC), the building became the organization's headquarters, housing the offices of its first president, Martin Luther King Jr. Other notable founders, members and staff included Andrew Young, Ella Baker, Ralph David Abernathy, Bayard Rustin, Dorothy Cotton, Joseph Lowery, C. T. Vivian, Diane Nash, James Bevel, Hosea Williams, Jesse Jackson, Septima Clark, and Fred Shuttlesworth, among others. After King's 1968 assassination, Rev. Abernathy became the SCLC's leader and continued operations at the lodge. The building also briefly served as a "shoppe" selling Madame C. J. Walker's beauty products, a powerful presence in twentieth century Sweet Auburn. In 2018, through the leadership of U.S. Representative John Lewis, a member of the Masons, the site was added to the Martin Luther King Jr. National

WERD
54 HILLIARD ST NE

Historical Park. The National Park Service and local funders are currently renovating the structure. The effort will restore and preserve the lodge's historic character and luster; upgrade its mechanical, electrical, and plumb-ing systems; and re-create King's office.

Atlanta University professor and bank president Jesse B. Blayton acquired radio station WERD 860 AM for $50,000 in 1949. It aired its inaugural broadcast from the Prince Hall Masonic Lodge on October 3 of that year, becoming the first Black-owned radio station in the United States. Disc jockey Jack Gibson, the Father of Black Appeal Radio, provided religious, music, sports, news, and other programming. Perhaps most important, WERD provided the SCLC with a megaphone for its civil rights activism, and King used the airwaves not only to broadcast Sunday sermons and encourage voter registration but also to rally, organize, and inform civil rights activists.

Sweet Auburn visitors can now view a reinvented radio studio created by Ricci de Forest (aka Ricci International), a creative soul and globally fluent fashion and beauty expert who exudes life and

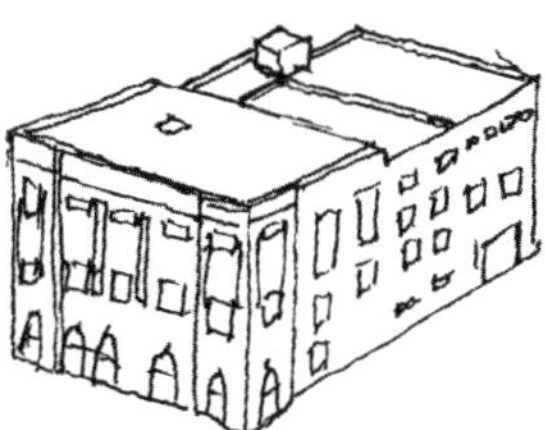

PRINCE HALL GRAND LODGE

energy. De Forest has been a mainstay of the lodge and an ambassador for Sweet Auburn since 2006, reimagining the shop that formerly sold Madame C. J. Walker's beauty products into a museum and event space that features a working beauty salon.

The woman who made a fortune as Madame C. J. Walker was born free as Sarah Breedlove in Louisiana in 1867. Orphaned by age seven and with only three months of formal education acquired at Sunday School, she developed a line of beauty and hair care products for Black women and became the first African American female self-made millionaire in the United States. Walker not only provided critical philanthropic support to education, religious, and civil rights causes but served as a role model, pointing the way to financial independence and equal rights for both African Americans and women.

In keeping with these many historical legacies, the Prince Hall Masonic Lodge will also continue to serve as a meeting place for the Masons as well as their female counterparts, the Eastern Stars.

# John Wesley Dobbs Plaza

**AUBURN AVENUE AT FORT STREET**

At the corner of Auburn Avenue and Fort Street sits a plaza designed to commemorate the life and leadership of the unofficial mayor of Sweet Auburn, John Wesley Dobbs. Dobbs was one of the earliest and most vocal champions of the neighborhood as a place where Black educational and commercial success could be translated into political power.

The plaza's focal point is a seven-foot bronze sculpture inspired by the twelfth-century Nigerian portrait mask tradition. Completed by sculptor Ralph Helmick in time for the 1996 Olympics, *Through His Eyes* depicts Dobbs looking out onto the community he loved. Helmick left open space in place of the eyes, allowing visitors to peer westward and catch Dobbs's vision. Dobbs's grandson, Atlanta mayor Maynard Jackson Jr., attended the artwork's dedication in 1996, highlighting the role of his grandfather's community-oriented activism in paving the way for Jackson's election.

Dobbs was born in 1882 in Marietta, Georgia, and grew up in a poor farming family in Kennesaw. He believed that "bucks, ballots, and books" could effect true emancipation for Black people. A voracious reader, Dobbs attended segregated public high school in Savannah before returning to the metro Atlanta area and attending Atlanta Baptist College (now Morehouse College). He left before graduating to care for his ailing mother. In 1903, Dobbs passed a civil

JOHN WESLEY
DOBBS PLAZA
FORT ST NE

service exam and was hired by the U.S. Post Office as a railway mail clerk, a position he held for thirty-two years.

Dobbs married Irene Ophelia Thompson in 1906, and the couple poured their educational fervor into their six daughters, all of whom graduated from Spelman College. Mattiwilda Dobbs was perhaps the most famous of the sisters, gaining international fame as a principal singer who toured Europe with the Metropolitan Opera. Irene Dobbs Jackson was the first Black person to obtain a library card that permitted her access to Atlanta's main public library system. She later taught French at Spelman, and her son Maynard became Atlanta's first Black mayor. June Dobbs Butts, the youngest of the Dobbs daughters, was an outspoken therapist and sexologist who is thought to have been the first Black woman to work with the Masters and Johnson Institute.

In seeking to solidify the community's educational foundations, John Wesley Dobbs partnered with groundbreakers such as Charles Lincoln Harper, the principal of the city's first Black public high school. Harper was a fearless youth advocate who also served as Sunday School superintendent at Sweet Auburn's Big Bethel AME Church. When Harper retired from Booker T. Washington High in 1942, the school's enrollment had grown to forty-two hundred. These pioneers understood that a solid education laid the groundwork for success in business, which they saw as fundamental prerequisites for political influence.

A charismatic leader, Dobbs was known to preach in the streets of Sweet Auburn about the right to vote—and whatever else caught his fancy. But on February 12, 1936, he used the pulpit at Big Bethel to give a rousing two-hour speech proposing the creation of the Atlanta Civic and Political League to register voters. Over the next ten years, the group helped to register nearly twenty thousand new Black voters—more than 25 percent of the Atlanta electorate. In 1946, Dobbs joined with A. T. Walden, a local power broker and lawyer who served as president of the Atlanta branch of the NAACP and represented it in civil rights cases alongside Thurgood Marshall, cofounded the Atlanta Negro Voters League.

These organizations delivered a sorely needed element of Black empowerment: influence in local elections. Politicians now had to pay attention to the Black community's needs or risk losing their jobs. This newfound responsiveness was made clear when Dobbs helped persuade Mayor William B. Hartsfield to hire the city's first eight Black police officers. Despite the well-documented hurdles faced by these pioneering officers both within the force and out on the streets, the move was a key step toward increasing Black participation in the city's power structure. The First Eight made their inaugural patrol on April 3, 1948, from the Butler Street YMCA, their segregated precinct: white officers were not yet ready to work directly with Black peers.

Dobbs's political influence came in large part from his role as the grand master of the state's Prince Hall Masons, an organization he had joined in 1911. The Grand, as he became known, led the organization from 1932 until his death in 1961. Not only did Dobbs build up the neighborhood from the Prince Hall Masonic Lodge at 330 Auburn, but he also literally built the lodge, leading construction between 1937 and 1941. Two of his daughters, June and Mattiwilda, placed a Bible with a four-leaf clover pressed between its pages in the cornerstone to honor Dobbs's persistent struggle.

"Bucks, ballots, and books" paid off: in 1956, *Fortune* magazine called Auburn Avenue "the richest Negro street in the world," nodding to the neighborhood's commerce, culture, and community. On August 30, 1961, the same week that the Atlanta city schools were integrated, Dobbs died at the age of seventy-nine. Martin Luther King Jr. spoke at the funeral, and Thurgood Marshall was a pallbearer.

Dobbs is buried at South-View Cemetery, the same hallowed grounds where U.S. Representative John Lewis, another influential Mason, is interred. Towering over Dobbs's final resting place is a fluted column—"square, plumb and level," in accordance with the Masons' motto—atop a stone base engraved with "Grand Master," a compass, and the dates marking his nearly three decades of service to the organization.

# Odd Fellows Building and Annex

**228-250 AUBURN AVENUE**

While the true origins of the Grand United Order of Odd Fellows are not definitively known, the society is said to have begun in England in the mid-eighteenth century. At that time, it was considered "odd" to find people organizing for the purpose of giving aid to strangers and endeavoring to benefit society without remuneration. By this measure, Sweet Auburn has certainly welcomed its share of enlightened eccentrics. Many of them found a home in the Odd Fellows Building, which was constructed in 1912 as the headquarters of the District Grand Lodge No. 18, with its Annex building opening next door a year later.

The Odd Fellows' American branch was organized by a group of freed Black people who petitioned to form their own group in 1842 after being rebuffed by white chapters. The following year, Peter Ogden, one of the order's Black members of British origins, sailed back home and obtained official permission to form the Philomathean Lodge No. 646 in New York. With that authorization, the Grand United Order of Odd Fellows in America was launched. It would become one of the largest and wealthiest Black fraternal orders in the United States.

Odd Fellow Benjamin Jefferson Davis Sr., considered by many to be Atlanta's most influential early Black journalist, conceived of the idea of locating the order's national headquarters on Auburn Avenue and

spearheaded the building's construction. "Big Ben" also founded the *Atlanta Independent*, the Black newspaper that amplified the opinionated editor's voice in the community for twenty-five years. Davis also amassed power as a patronage leader within the Republican Party, using the complementary platforms of paper and politics to build consensus for the cause of Black prosperity and civil rights.

Fashioned of red brick, terra-cotta, and stone, the Odd Fellows tower and Annex buildings were designed in the Jacobean Revival style by renowned Atlanta architect William Augustus Edwards. A white man from South Carolina, Edwards designed stunning courthouses and educational buildings across the South in the early 1900s. The National Register of Historic Places lists more than twenty-five of his works, among them not only the Odd Fellows block but also the intricately decorated Buttrick Hall at Agnes Scott College, an extraordinary example of collegiate Gothic architecture just up the road in Decatur.

The six-story Odd Fellows tower was built for $250,000 by Robert E. Pharrow, a prolific contractor who worked on many of Sweet Auburn's historic churches, including the First

Congregational Church, United Church of Christ, at the intersection of John Wesley Dobbs Avenue and Courtland Street, as well as Wheat Street Baptist Church. The Odd Fellows tower included space for the order's meetings, offices for Black-owned businesses and professional service providers, and street-level retail space. At its dedication, Booker T. Washington heralded the building as a standard-bearer for Black ingenuity.

The two-story Annex building (also known as the Auditorium) included an open atrium, bringing an early dash of entertainment and culture to augment the tower's business bent. A stone-carved ribbon above the Annex's front door is inscribed with the letters *F, L,* and *T* to signify Friendship, Love, and Truth. Built for $100,000 in 1913, the year after Paramount Pictures was founded and Thomas Edison produced the first talking motion picture, the Annex accommodated thirteen hundred guests for meetings (including the order's national conventions) and housed Bailey's Royal Theatre, the only Atlanta theater where Blacks were allowed to sit on the main level rather than segregated in the balcony. The Annex's rooftop garden was also known for recreational refinement: in the 1920s and 1930s it hosted storied dance parties with entertainment by legends such as Count Basie, Cab Calloway, Bessie Smith, and Lionel Hampton.

In 1914, Dr. Moses Amos, Georgia's first Black pharmacist, opened the Gate City Drug Store on the ground level of the Annex. According to the *Atlanta Independent,* it was at the time one of the largest Black drugstores in the world. In 1924, under new ownership, it was renamed Yates & Milton Drugs. Other businesses on the Odd Fellows block included the House of Flowers, Sportsman's Smoke House, the Curry-Hall Haberdasher, and the Gate City Barber Shop.

The Great Depression brought rising debts and budget cuts, and the Odd Fellows Building and Annex were sold in the early 1930s. Fire damaged the building in 1937, and multiple owners subsequently tried and failed to resurrect the bygone era. The buildings were sold for a mere $5,000 in 1943. Over the next four decades, white flight and the long, hard fall of Sweet Auburn led the buildings to fall into disrepair.

The Odd Fellows Building launched its comeback in 1975, when it was listed on the National Register of Historic Places. In 1987, architect Robert "Skip" Perkins and his wife, Janis, brought the property back under Black ownership and began a restoration. Skip Perkins died in 1990, and Janis Perkins finished the project the following year. The move not only was important for the buildings' history but also served as a landmark moment in Sweet Auburn's preservation, a visible way of providing the community with Friendship, Love, and Truth.

Today, the Annex once again hosts professional offices and retail shops, including one near and dear to the heart of former president Bill Clinton: Sweet Auburn Bread Company, which he visited while in office in 1999. Owned by Chef Sonya Jones, it bakes in the love and traditions of yesteryear while still being very much of today. Chef favorites include buttermilk-lemon chess pies, sweet potato–molasses muffins, and pecan brownies.

Try the sweet potato cheesecake, as Clinton did. It's said to be presidential.

# Gold Dust Twins and the Atlanta Life Local Branch

**229 AUBURN AVENUE (EAST SIDE)**

**THE HERNDON BUILDING**
**229-243 AUBURN AVENUE**

On March 14, 2008, a tornado tore through downtown Atlanta, barreling up Auburn Avenue from Centennial Olympic Park along a six-mile path of destruction, concluding its furious course near a devastated Oakland Cemetery. Notable buildings such as the Westin Peachtree Plaza, the Georgia World Congress Center, the Omni Hotel, the CNN Center, the Fulton Cotton Mill Lofts, the Southern School Book Building and the *Atlanta Daily World* Building sustained damage to the tune of $250 million. In addition to the loss of property, the storm exacerbated existing hurdles to preservation in Sweet Auburn. But the resulting demolitions also unearthed a long-concealed reminder of the continuing need to press for racial equity.

Battered beyond repair was the historic Herndon Building at 229–243 Auburn Avenue, a substantial L-shaped complex completed in 1924. The four-story building housed sixty offices for Black professionals along with six street-level retail storefronts. Included in the complex were the thirty-four-room Savoy Hotel, the offices of the Atlanta Urban League and the NAACP, the Atlanta School of Social Work, and the Galanti Brothers Delicatessen. The property also featured underground parking, which at the time of construction was a prophetic nod to the city's growing car culture.

Gold Dust
229 Auburn Ave NE

Originally attached to the Herndon Building and also badly damaged was a three-story structure housing the Atlanta Life Branch Office a few blocks east of the company's headquarters on Auburn Avenue at Piedmont. When the Herndon Building was torn down a month after the tornado, a long-obscured sign on the eastern face of the Atlanta Life Branch Office at the corner of Auburn and Jesse Hill Jr. Drive became visible. Still visible today, this "ghost sign" hearkens back to a disturbing era in American commerce, when Black citizens were no longer enslaved but were still forced to endure visual reminders of their subservience. The Gold Dust Twins advertisement is believed to have been painted no later than 1924 and offers a graphic reminder of a tarnished past.

The Gold Dust Twins originally appeared in 1887 advertisements for N. K. Fairbank's Gold Dust Washing Powder. Drawn by E. W. Kimble, the staff artist of the *Chicago Daily Graphic*, the characters started to gain widespread recognition at the 1904 St. Louis World's Fair. Early ads placed in the *Atlanta Constitution* urged white housewives to "Let the Gold Dust Twins Do Your Work," with dark-skinned Goldie and Dustie ready to serve. Based on caricatures still prevalent at the turn of the century, the twins offer a grotesque reminder of how Blacks were viewed, treated, and displayed to the public—a second act of commercial exploitation just a few decades after the horrors of slavery. From an advertising standpoint, the illustration was wildly successful, leading to a radio program featuring actors portraying the twins and spurring minstrel shows featuring blackface performers.

Lever Brothers purchased the Gold Dust brand during the 1930s and discontinued it after World War II, in part because of competition from other products and in part because of rising national distaste for racist marketing. That distaste, combined with the increasing power of the Civil Rights Movement beginning in the mid-1950s, led most advertisers to quietly move away from these types of discriminatory ads, though some, such as Aunt Jemima, persisted for decades longer. Though Gold Dust Washing Powder itself is long gone, on Auburn Avenue,the Gold Dust Twins continue to push their product to passersby, a reminder of work left to be done and of important lessons that must be imparted to future generations.

# Big Bethel African Methodist Episcopal (AME) Church

### 220 AUBURN AVENUE

Big Bethel African Methodist Episcopal (AME) Church is the oldest Black church in Sweet Auburn. It sprang out of Union Church, a white congregation that allowed a contingent of enslaved Black congregants to worship starting in 1847. In 1855, this small group, led by founding pastor Joseph Woods, split off to form Bethel Tabernacle and opened its first building. The church became known as Big Bethel in 1865, when it joined the fast-growing AME denomination. Steady growth culminated in the construction of the handsome Victorian-style stone church building at the corner of Wheat and Butler Streets (now Auburn Avenue and Jesse Hill Jr. Drive), which opened in 1891.

Hailed as Sweet Auburn's City Hall, the church served as a nexus for social action, community organizing, and educational outreach. Gate City Colored School, established in the basement in 1879, was one of a handful of early schools providing free education to Black students in the city. Similarly, the AME Church's Morris Brown College, the first college in Georgia organized solely by Black people, began holding classes in Big Bethel's basement in 1881 and stayed there until the school's first permanent campus opened four years later.

Big Bethel's membership swelled after the Great Fire of 1917 destroyed all of the Fourth Ward's other Black churches. Ironically, the same force that helped propel the church nearly destroyed it just a few years later. In 1923, an inferno engulfed the newly renovated sanctuary just one day after its insurance policy lapsed. With the church forced to rebuild, Black architect J. A. Lankford offered a new vision and destiny with a Romanesque Revival design that reflected the church's Victorian roots. A signature steeple and pipe organ were added during the reconstruction.

Resurrecting the congregation's spiritual home required faith and perseverance in the face of financial hardship. Lula B. Jones and Nellie L. Davis, who sang in the church choir and taught at its Sunday School, sought to raise funds by selling tickets to a play they wrote that was accompanied by spirituals and hymns. Their prayers were answered several times over: *Heaven Bound* debuted at Big Bethel on February 17, 1930, and went on to enjoy overwhelming success both at home and on tour, where it had been performed before more than one million people by the early 1970s.

The playwrights saw heaven as a religious metaphor for the pursuit of freedom by enslaved people. Even with its overt messages of racial justice, *Heaven Bound* drew illegally integrated audiences of fifteen hundred for its annual Atlanta performances, becoming what the *New York Times* called "one of Atlanta's most enduring traditions" and the Theatre Guild hailed as the "first great American folk drama."[1] The show's choir performed for President Franklin D. Roosevelt at the Little White House in Warm Springs, Georgia, and at the world premiere of *Gone with the Wind* in 1939 at Atlanta's Loew's Grand Theater. (Some choir members were permitted to stay and watch the premiere, although cast members such as Hattie McDaniel, who won an Oscar for her performance as Mammy, were not invited.) Performances of *Heaven Bound* continue today, making the production one of the longest-lasting in U.S. history.

BIG BETHEL
220 AUBURN AVE NE
JESUS
SAVES

On February 12, 1936, John Wesley Dobbs used Big Bethel's pulpit to call for the formation of the Atlanta Civic and Political League, an effort to register ten thousand Black voters. Over the next decade, twice that number were added to the rolls, an early invocation of Black political power and an appeal to civic engagement that proved foundational to the Civil Rights Movement.

In addition to its designation as a historical landmark, Big Bethel continues to function as an active AME congregation, welcoming members, visitors, and a flow of students from nearby Georgia State University every Sunday. The church's notable architectural features include stained-glass windows featuring likenesses of Bishops Richard Allen (founder of the AME church), Henry M. Turner, and Joseph S. Flipper, and an iconic illuminated blue "Jesus Saves" sign visible to motorists on the Downtown Connector.

Along with dynamic church leaders, other prominent figures who have spoken from the pulpit include Booker T. Washington, President William Howard Taft, Mary McLeod Bethune, Dr. Martin Luther King Jr., President Jimmy Carter, Nelson Mandela, and President Bill Clinton.

BIG BETHEL

# John Lewis HERO Mural

**SOUTHWEST CORNER OF AUBURN AVENUE AND JESSE HILL JR. DRIVE**

The John Lewis HERO Mural honors one of Atlanta's most resolute and impassioned voices for freedom. It stands tall as a landmark for the Fifth Congressional District, which Lewis served from 1987 until his death on July 17, 2020.

When Lewis died, leaving broken hearts all over the city and around the world, the mural quickly became a memorial site where hundreds came to pay their respects by leaving flowers, letters, and prayers in his honor. This outpouring of grief and respect showed that the space was and is more than just a significant and beautiful work of art: it is a reminder, a motivator, and now a monument for posterity to a stalwart leader of the Civil Rights Movement who stood firm against injustice and inequality.

The John Lewis HERO Mural was created in 2012 by Sean Schwab and Maggie White of the Loss Prevention in collaboration with Matt Weyandt and other members of Representative Lewis's staff and with support from Jennifer Ball and A. J. Robinson of Central Atlanta Progress. It was brought to fruition in Sweet Auburn with the help and leadership of Gene Kansas | Commercial Real Estate.

In a 2012 interview, Lewis explained connections among art, freedom, and the movement:

JOHN LEWIS MURAL
219 AUBURN AVE
*HERO
"I APPEAL TO ALL OF YOU TO GET INTO THIS GREAT REVOLUTION THAT IS SWEEPING THIS NATION. GET IN AND STAY IN THE STREETS OF EVERY CITY, EVERY VILLAGE AND HAMLET OF THIS NATION UNTIL TRUE FREEDOM COMES, UNTIL THE REVOLUTION OF 1776 IS COMPLETE."
-JOHN LEWIS

> Without the arts, without the painting, sculpt[ure] pieces, the drawings, without music, dance, theater, or whatever you want to call it, the Civil Rights Movement would have been like a bird without wings. Somehow and some way, artists were able to tell us something about the distance we've come, about our past, our present, but also about our future. [Art] moves people in different ways and different forms. It may move you to laugh or just to smile. It may move you to cry and shed some tears. But it could move you to stand up and make you more determined to engage in a struggle to make things better for all humankind.
>
> The only thing it takes to be a voice for freedom is to be prepared and be willing to speak up for the freedom of all humankind. When you see something that is not right, something not fair, not just, when you see people being mistreated, a people being held down because of their class, their race, their religion or national origin, you have a moral obligation to do something, to find a way to change things.
>
> There will always be a cost, a price to pay to be free. When I was much younger, as a teenager, I heard the words of Martin Luther King Jr. on my old radio. It seemed like he was speaking directly to me, and I wanted to do something about what I saw. And when my mother and father heard that I was sitting in at lunch counters or going on the Freedom Rides, they thought that I was going to get hurt or maybe killed. They told me not to get in trouble, don't get in trouble, but I got in trouble. It was good trouble. It was necessary trouble. And I think not just because of what I tried to do but what hundreds and thousands and millions of citizens, Black and white, Latinos, Asian Americans, and Native Americans tried to do, our country is a better country, and we are a freer country. But we're not truly there yet; we still have work to do.[1]

On July 30, 2021, nine years after the mural was unveiled and one year after Lewis's passing, Central Atlanta Progress organized a rededication ceremony that featured remarks from civic leader

Andrew Young, former gubernatorial candidate Stacey Abrams, and Natalyn Archibong and Amir Farokhi of the Atlanta City Council. Ebenezer Baptist Church's Christine King Farris Handbell Choir played during a community-wide moment of reflection. Toward the end of the program, author and cultural developer Gene Kansas offered personal reflections about the representative and thoughts on what a rededication might look like. As a nod to Lewis's words on the link between creativity and freedom, Kansas advocated increasing arts and culture programming in the community and constructing a plaza for peace in what is now a parking lot in front of the mural.

The Butler Street Community Development Corporation and Central Atlanta Progress are now in the process of planning a small memorial park where visitors can pay tribute to and celebrate the civil rights leader and national hero.

Lewis is buried at South-View Cemetery, where his tombstone reads, "They walked where others had not gone."

# Butler Street YMCA

## 22 JESSE HILL JR. DRIVE

The naming of city streets often becomes a battleground of memory, an exercise in revisionism creating conflict over the moments and people we collectively decide are important enough to recall. When Butler Drive was renamed Jesse Hill Jr. Drive in 2001, however, the change did not overwrite a past legacy; it simply honored one man who carried on the ideals of another pioneer who paved the way.

Embedded in the story of two names attributed to one thoroughfare intersecting Auburn Avenue is a tale of business acumen and a hunger for knowledge that is integral to Sweet Auburn's reputation as a place where ideas ignite transformative action.

The street's initial namesake was Sweet Auburn forefather Henry Rutherford Butler, a doctor, pharmacist, and civic leader who arrived in Atlanta in 1890 from Tennessee. Henry and his wife, Selena Sloan Butler, a Spelman College graduate and an educator and luminary in her own right, constructed an astounding legacy starting at the crossroads that later carried their name.

Henry Butler's achievements were all the more impressive given his humble beginnings. Born enslaved in 1862, in the thick of the Civil War, he was raised in the North Carolina countryside and received no formal schooling. Butler worked at hotels and mills and was tutored in the evenings. He went on to earn a diploma from Lincoln University in Pennsylvania before graduating from Nashville's Meharry Medical College in 1890. The following year, Butler and a Meharry classmate opened a drugstore and doctor's office on Atlanta's Wheat Street. The drugstore later came under the ownership of Moses Amos, the state's first Black pharmacist, and in 1914 it became Gate City Drugs, located in the Odd Fellows Building just across from Big Bethel AME Church, where the Butlers were devout members.

In addition to his medical practice, Butler was also a prolific promoter of his profession, advancing Black practitioners' roles in the field of medicine by bringing researchers and physicians together over his four-decade career. He cofounded the Atlanta Medical Association in 1890 and just three years later helped establish a statewide association. Expanding his reach and his contributions even further, Butler joined with other leaders to found the National Medical Association, the African American counterpart to the American Medical Association, which refused to admit Black physicians, during the 1895 Cotton States and International Exposition, which brought widespread attention to Atlanta in part thanks to Booker T. Washington's promotional efforts.

In 1887, Butler enrolled in Meharry Medical College in Nashville, Tennessee, graduating with a medical degree three years later. Continuing his pursuit and passion, Butler eventually become dean of the School of Nursing at Morris Brown College, which had been founded in the basement of Big Bethel, where he served as a steward. Butler's activism included writing articles for the *Atlanta Independent* and the *Atlanta Constitution* as well as a thirty-year stint as grand master of the Prince Hall Grand Lodge of Georgia, starting in 1901. When Butler died in 1931, he was succeeded by John Wesley Dobbs, who served for the next three decades and became known as the Grand.

Selena Sloan Butler, born in 1872, was also an organizer. As an outgrowth of her work at Atlanta's Yonge Street Elementary School,

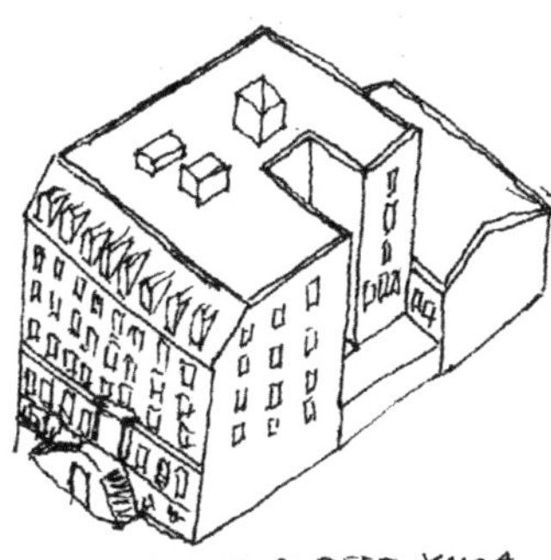


where her son Henry Jr. was enrolled, she founded the National Congress of Colored Parents and Teachers as a counterpart to the white Parent-Teacher Association. When the two groups merged under the name National Parent-Teacher Association after Butler's 1964 death, the new organization named her one of its founders. She was a city and state leader in the National Association of Colored Women, which led the Black clubwomen's movement. During World War II, she joined Henry Jr., also a physician, in Arizona, where she founded the first Black chapter of the Gray Ladies, volunteers who assisted the Red Cross with its work. Selena Sloan Butler's papers are archived at the Auburn Avenue Research Library on African American Culture and History, and her portrait is on display in the Georgia Capitol. The couple is buried in Oakland Cemetery.

The Butlers were members of the Commission on Interracial Cooperation, an antilynching and race-reform group founded in Atlanta in 1918 that brought together Blacks and whites, part of their decades-long commitment to enhancing the well-being of African American children and students. Fittingly, therefore, the Butler Street Young Men's Christian Association (YMCA) stood for a long time as the best-known Atlanta landmark carrying their name.

Founded in the basement of Wheat Street Baptist Church by J. S. Brandon in 1894, the YMCA found a permanent home on Butler Street in 1920. A pillar of the Civil Rights Movement, the Butler Street YMCA became known as the Black City Hall of Atlanta, reflecting its role as a kingmaker in the city's political power structure and as a mecca for leadership in both the Black and white communities.

Built between 1916 and 1920 by Alexander D. Hamilton, a Black contractor responsible for many Sweet Auburn's structures, the 37,600-square-foot brick building was designed by Neel Reid of Hentz, Reid & Adler in a customized version of the Georgian Revival style that brought the firm widespread acclaim. As was standard for YMCAs of the time, Butler Street was intended for housing, recreation, and community programming and consequently featured dorm rooms, a swimming pool, a gymnasium, and meeting space.

At Butler Street, boys came to play and men were made. Among those who grew up swimming in the pool, sharing meals at the lunch counter, playing basketball, and mixing, mingling, and debating within the building's walls were Martin Luther King Jr.; renowned business and civic leader Jesse Hill Jr.; Vernon Jordan, a civil rights activist and adviser to President Bill Clinton; National Basketball Association great Walt "Clyde" Frazier; and Atlanta's first Black mayor, Maynard Jackson Jr. As adults in positions of power, these men and others cut from the same cloth kept the Butler Street Y at the center of Atlanta's civic and social life. Beginning in 1948, the Y served as the precinct for the city's first eight Black policemen, who were barred from serving at the force's downtown headquarters.

The exchange of dialogue and ideas at the Y was no accident. In 1945, author Ira D. Reid, chair of the sociology department at Atlanta

University (later merged with Clark College to form Clark Atlanta University), decided that the city needed a forum for frank and honest debate across racial lines. A simple but radical idea at a time of great racial division, the Hungry Club Forum began as a secret society that met in the basement of the Butler Street YMCA, offering southern food and stirring conversation each Wednesday from noon to 1:30 when the public schools were in session. In 1950, a broader audience gained access to the club when Sweet Auburn's WERD, the first Black-owned radio station in the United States, began broadcasting the Hungry Club's Wednesday programs. The Hungry Club became a fixture on the air and in the basement for the next seven decades.

The program featured speeches followed by open dialogue and was moderated by William A. Fowlkes of the *Atlanta Daily World* newspaper. Lucille Scott, widow of *Atlanta Daily World* founder William Alexander Scott, served as host, adding further prominence to the family business as a vehicle for reporting on and cultivating Black culture from Sweet Auburn.

Many exceptional orators participated over the decades, with the sitting mayor customarily kicking off each new year. In 1981, Mayor Maynard Jackson Jr. provided spirited support for former U.S. ambassador to the United Nations Andrew Young in his runoff mayoral election against white opponent Sidney Marcus. Jackson lambasted Black voters who favored Marcus, causing an uproar that garnered national media attention. Young prevailed.

Long before that pivotal moment, white mayors of Atlanta had acknowledged the Butler Street Y's sphere of influence, especially after 1944, when the U.S. Supreme Court outlawed all-white primaries, by seeking counsel and votes there. Incumbent mayor William B. Hartsfield made his first visit to the Y shortly after the ruling, encouraging Black people to register to vote (and, by implication, to cast their ballots for him). Over the next few months, eighteen thousand new names were added to the rolls, thanks in no small part to the Butler Street Y's efforts. Those voters then helped Hartsfield not only win reelection but remain in office until 1962, making Black City Hall a mandatory stop for politicians. Mayor Ivan Allen Jr., who succeeded the retiring Hartsfield in 1962, went to the Butler Street Y to gather opinions on the congressional testimony he would offer as the only southern elected official to publicly back the Civil Rights Act of 1964.

In 2011, with the crumbling Butler Street Y unavailable for use, Mayor Kasim Reed delivered the Hungry Club's final mayoral speech at Georgia State University's Dahlberg Hall. The Hungry Club Forum ended the following year, just as a new and uncertain chapter for the Butler Street building began.

Among the Butler Street Y members most eager for knowledge, justice, and commercial success was Jesse Hill Jr., an exceptional leader and a bridge between Atlanta's Black and white business communities. Hill earned a graduate degree at the University of Michigan and moved to Atlanta in 1949, initially residing in a dorm room at the Butler Street Y. Hill quickly impressed the city's business community, becoming the second Black actuary in the United States. His first and only employer was Atlanta Life Insurance Company: he ultimately became its president and CEO (1973–92), the first executive outside of founder Alonzo Herndon's immediate family to hold that position. An early riser, Hill issued orders, scheduled meetings, and made phone calls just after dawn, before the other participants were fully awake.

Under Hill's leadership, Atlanta Life became the largest privately held Black business in the United States. Putting his political

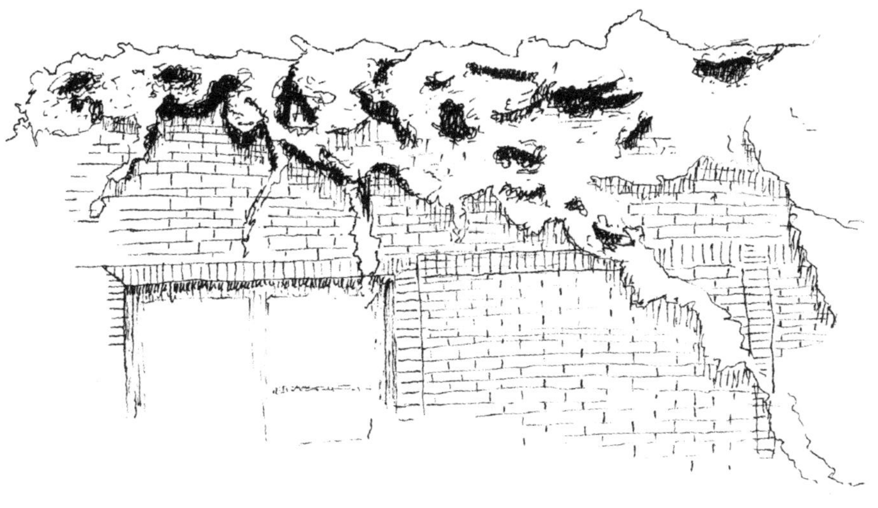

power, community standing, and pocketbook to good use, Hill became a torchbearer for the Civil Rights Movement and its broader economic and political ideals. Leveraging the company's platform, Hill provided Black customers in Georgia and beyond with wider access to affordable residential mortgages. In 1973, he became the first Black member of the University System of Georgia's Board of Regents. Three years later, he became the first Black chamber of commerce president in a major American city, and he subsequently became the first Black board member of Rich's Department Store. He also served as longtime chair of the board of the Martin Luther King Jr. Center, tenaciously fundraising for King and the cause. Hill also hired Rosa Parks, the Mother of the Freedom Movement, as a secretary at Atlanta Life after her civil disobedience arrest that led to the Montgomery Bus Boycott.

Hill helped facilitate the desegregation of Atlanta's public schools and Georgia's universities. As a founding director of MARTA, he helped make possible public transportation on a major scale. Politically connected, Hill ran successful mayoral campaigns for Jackson and

BUTLER STREET YMCA
22 JESSE HILL JR DR NE

Young. In 1970, Hill helped Muhammad Ali stage a comeback fight in Atlanta in the face of his legal troubles with the federal government, a bout that resurrected his career. The champ returned to the city twenty-six years later, lighting the Olympic Cauldron to officially welcome the world to the 1996 Summer Olympic Games. Hill was instrumental in bringing them to the city as well.

In 2001, the City of Atlanta changed Butler Street's name to Jesse Hill Jr. Drive. When Hill died in 2012 at age eighty-six, U.S. Representative John Lewis said that Hill had "envisioned Atlanta as a cornerstone in the South of a transformed and renewed America. And he did more than dream, but he worked to make that vision a reality."[1] A mural of Lewis graces a towering wall next to the Butler Street YMCA and watches over Jesse Hill Jr. Drive.

Also in 2012, deteriorating conditions and the lack of a focused and funded preservation effort forced closure of the Butler Street YMCA after 118 years of progress and pride. Ownership transferred to the Butler Street Community Development Corporation, a holding company. The structure remains closed, in peril of demolition or collapse, but at least for now, it still stands as a testament to an astonishing history of dialogue and dynamism.

What was once one of the greatest galvanizing forces in Atlanta history is now endangered by what preservationists call demolition via neglect, as is its landmark neighbor, the Atlanta Life Branch Office just across Jesse Hill Jr. Drive.

Given that the street's current namesake made his living at Atlanta Life, those working to preserve the landmark building bearing Butler's name would do well to consider the intersection holistically, continuing to honor both monumental men who paved the way for the city's inclusive, lasting growth.

Y·M·C·A

## AN OVERVIEW

*The area surrounding the intersection of Piedmont and Auburn Avenues was the commercial and cultural heart of this vibrant neighborhood, a place where history was made and the ability to make it was accessible. These pages introduce some of the colorful characters and groundbreaking businesses that made Auburn sweet, strong, and forward-looking.*

*In this chapter, you'll find musical and financial independence, First Amendment pioneers, a stunning library dedicated to African American history, one of the world's leading mentor organizations, and remarkable stories about entrepreneurial icons.*

*Leaders from the more modern era include a contemporary cultural center in a historic building and the country's top school for awarding bachelor's degrees to African Americans. This section of Sweet Auburn truly represents a cornerstone of the community.*

CHAPTER 4

# AUBURN AT PIEDMONT

*A Cornerstone of Music, Financial Independence, and Knowledge*

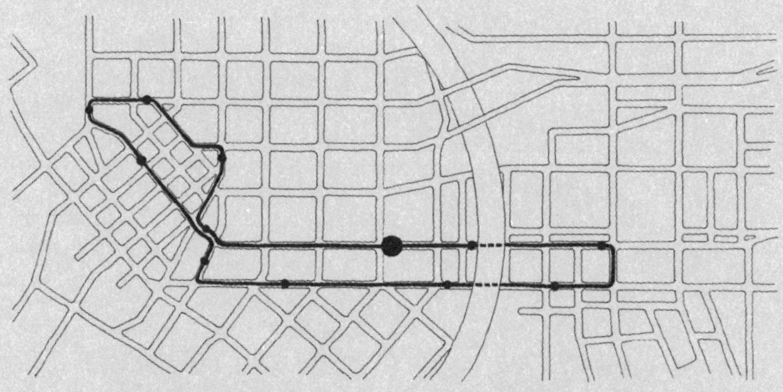

ATLANTA STREETCAR STOP: AUBURN AT PIEDMONT

**THE ROYAL PEACOCK**
186 AUBURN AVENUE

**CITIZENS TRUST BANK**
75 PIEDMONT AVENUE

**ATLANTA DAILY WORLD BUILDING**
145 AUBURN AVENUE

**100 BLACK MEN OF AMERICA**
141 AUBURN AVENUE

**ATLANTA LIFE INSURANCE COMPANY**
142-148 AUBURN AVENUE

**SOUTHERN SCHOOL BOOK BUILDING**
135 AUBURN AVENUE

**CENTENNIAL HALL**
100 AUBURN AVENUE

**AUBURN AVENUE RESEARCH LIBRARY ON AFRICAN AMERICAN CULTURE AND HISTORY**
101 AUBURN AVENUE

# The Royal Peacock

## 186 AUBURN AVENUE

The Royal Peacock originally opened on the upper level of 186 Auburn Avenue as the Top Hat Club in 1937, some eight years after construction of the Egyptian Revival structure with multiple ground-level storefronts. As a standard stop on the Chitlin' Circuit, a string of venues providing platforms for Black artists during segregation, the club attracted an impressive roster of performers, including superstars such as B. B. King, Gladys Knight, Little Richard, Sam Cooke, Miles Davis, Ray Charles, Jackie Wilson, Fats Domino, the Four Tops, Dizzy Gillespie, Otis Redding, Dinah Washington, Marvin Gaye, and Stevie Wonder.

Flamboyant former circus rider Carrie "Mama" Cunningham bought the Top Hat in 1949, renaming it the Royal Peacock and updating the decor to match, with plumed wallpaper, murals of the regal bird, and lavish feather arrays streaming from the facade. Known popularly and on its neon signage as Atlanta's Club Beautiful, the venue was a favorite of well-heeled Black audiences as well as whites, especially during its twice-weekly "whites-only" evenings. The racial diversity of the Royal Peacock's clientele laid the groundwork for the integration of Atlanta nightlife and the ascendancy of Black music in the broader culture. The fire marshal officially limited occupancy at 350, although hundreds more reportedly packed the house during the club's heyday, with throngs of smartly dressed patrons stretching around the block on their way

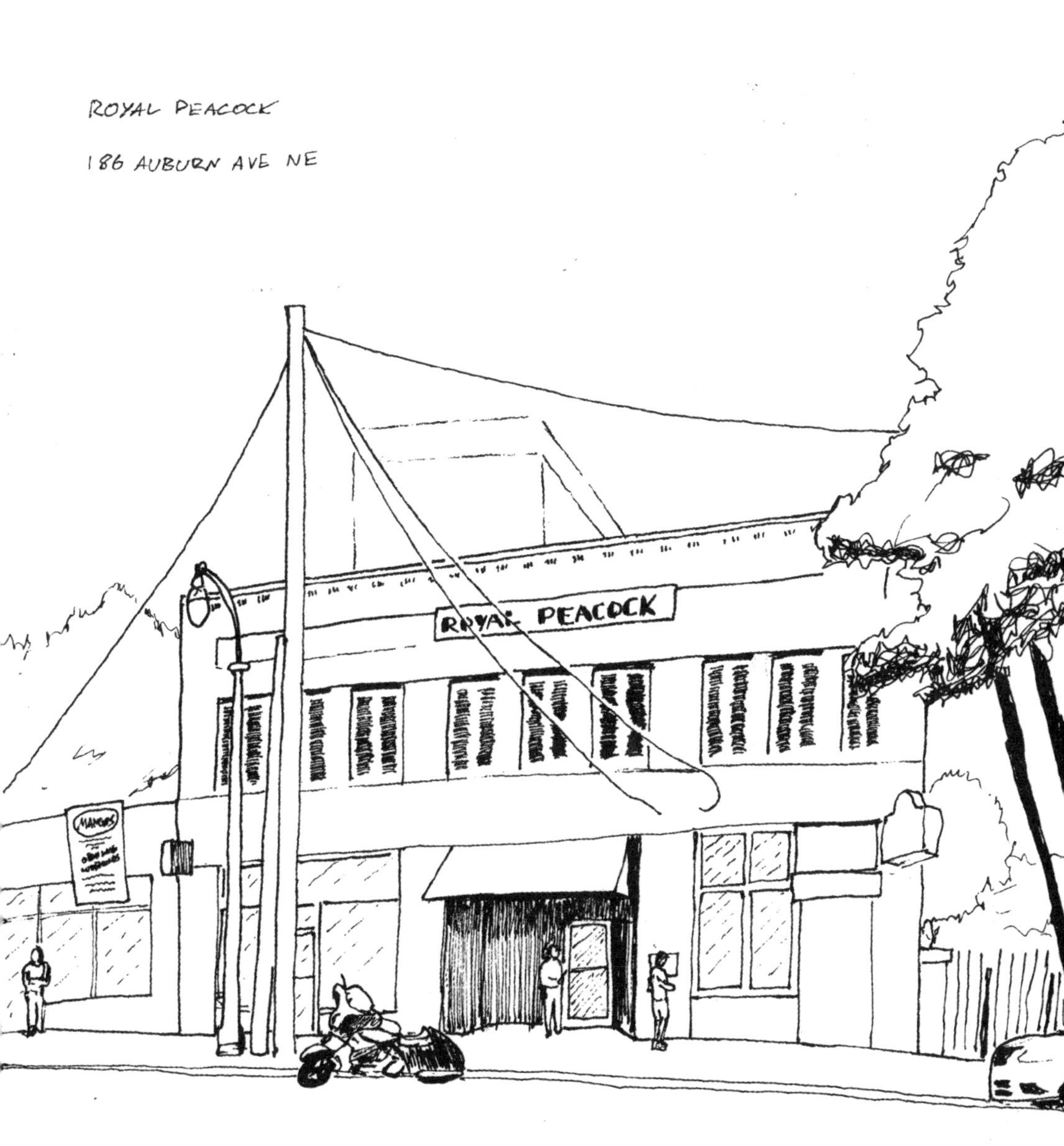
ROYAL PEACOCK
186 AUBURN AVE NE
ROYAL PEACOCK

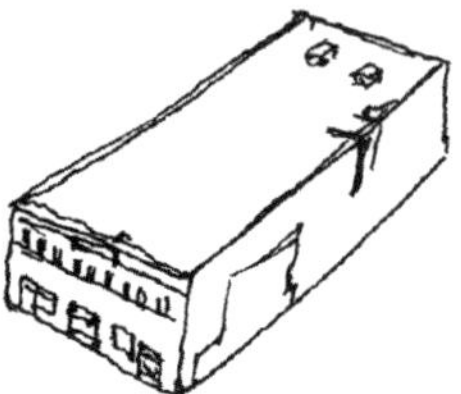

ROYAL PEACOCK

in. Admission was typically $3.50 for what some called the South's answer to Harlem's famed Apollo Theater. Reminiscing in the *Atlanta Journal-Constitution,* Aretha Franklin said that the club was "as hot as it could get" and acknowledged frequenting Henry's Grill next door. Muhammad Ali took in an evening blues performance at the Royal Peacock in February 1964 before taking the heavyweight boxing crown from Sonny Liston the next day in Miami.

Mama Cunningham also ran the nearby Royal Hotel and Restaurant, a refuge of rest and refinement for Black performers and others barred from white establishments during this era. The hotel, listed in *The Negro Travelers' Green Book: The Guide to Travel and Vacations,* was situated on the upper levels of the original Citizens Trust Bank building adjacent to and owned by Big Bethel Church. After the bank relocated to new headquarters just up Piedmont Avenue in the 1960s, the building was demolished and ultimately became a parking deck.

The Royal Peacock still struts today in its current incarnation as a reggae spot. Despite the building's gradual decline and at least one three-alarm fire, the building stands as a lingering memorial to the club's outsized and brilliant influence in making Atlanta a music hub and providing a symbolic soundtrack for the Civil Rights Movement.

# Citizens Trust Bank

## 75 PIEDMONT AVENUE

Led by entrepreneur Heman E. Perry, Citizens Trust Bank was founded in 1919 by a group of visionaries known as the Fervent Five. When a white store owner refused to fit Perry for socks, he came up with the idea of starting a bank to foster Black independence from white-owned lenders and businesses.

Perry, the bank's first board chair, recruited a rock-solid executive team that included James A. Robinson, Thomas J. Ferguson, W. H. King, and H. C. Dugas; Dugas became the bank's first president. Together, they created a financial anchor for the Sweet Auburn community that eventually grew into one of the largest Black-owned banks in the United States, now with more than $400 million in assets.

Citizens Trust opened its doors on August 12, 1921, at 210 Auburn Avenue. The bank started with $500,000 in capital invested toward the goals of financial stability, thrift, and homeownership in the Black community. The bank's reliability faced an early test on February 16, 1923, when fire engulfed Big Bethel Church. The church, a cornerstone of Sweet Auburn that also owned the building where the bank operated, turned to Citizens Trust for reconstruction funding. The partnership foretold the bank's future as a preferred lender to pivotal Atlanta houses of worship: in 1998,

CITIZENS TRUST BANK
75 PIEDMONT AVE NE C
CITIZENS TRUST BANK

Ebenezer Baptist Church borrowed $5.5 million from the bank to build its new sanctuary.

In addition to preserving history, Citizens Trust Company made some of its own in 1934, when it became the first Black-owned member of the budding Federal Deposit Insurance Corporation. In 1948, ten years after Lorimer D. Milton was promoted from treasurer to president and CEO, Citizens Trust became the first Black-owned bank to join the Federal Reserve System.

In the midst of the Civil Rights Movement, the bank opened its Westside Branch, a move that reflected the vision and management skill of that generation of its leaders, whose board of directors in the 1950s and 1960s included Dr. Benjamin E. Mays, president of Morehouse College, and the Reverend Martin Luther King Sr. of Ebenezer Baptist Church. Under their guidance, the bank invested in development loans for housing subdivisions in southwest Atlanta. Like Sweet Auburn, these neighborhoods were places where Black residents of Atlanta could overcome discriminatory practices like redlining that kept them from realizing the American Dream.

Economic opportunity with financial independence was not merely a hallmark of Citizens Trust Bank but *was and remains* its mission. Providing guidance and funding to individuals and businesses during the Civil Rights Movement led to blossoming returns on investment for Black banks as the movement found success. Greater national support for the cause also enabled people of color to gain home equity and build wealth, particularly when presidential leadership resulted in policy change.

The assassination of John F. Kennedy on November 22, 1963, was a tragic moment in history and a petrifying moment in time.

The event hurled the country into mourning and shocked appalled citizens into action. Kennedy's successor, Lyndon B. Johnson, not only sought to carry forward the slain president's civil rights agenda but also launched the Great Society, an ambitious legislative effort aimed at ending poverty. Many Great Society programs eliminated discriminatory practices in support of the goal of fundamental, long-lasting, and transformative social reform.

In his January 1964 State of the Union address, with an eye on reelection, Johnson announced an "unconditional war on poverty." Further leveraging executive power, Johnson followed up with his March 16 "Special Message to Congress," in which he introduced the Economic Opportunity Act of 1964, an encompassing initiative with a focus on social welfare that unofficially became known as the War on Poverty.

In his address to Congress Johnson proclaimed: "This program will show the way to new opportunities for millions of our fellow citizens. It will provide a lever with which we can begin to open the door to our prosperity for those who have been kept outside." He explained, "Through a new Community Action program we intend to strike at poverty at its source—in the streets of our cities and on the farms of our countryside among the very young and the impoverished old. This program asks men and women throughout the country to prepare long-range plans for the attack on poverty in their own local communities."[1]

Johnson's action created job, education, and training programs and provided business and home loans for hundreds of thousands of citizens, helping tilt the scales toward equality. To administer and lead the effort, dozens of Black banks and many more credit unions opened to serve the expanding client base. By the time the War on Poverty was signed into law in August 1964, Citizens

Trust Bank had been purposefully planning and implementing financial independence for more than forty years. With support from the federal government, Black people in Sweet Auburn and well beyond became for the first time the deserving beneficiaries of broader lending opportunities.

A month earlier, Johnson had signed into law the Civil Rights Act of 1964, prohibiting discrimination on the basis of race, color, religion, sex, or national origin. And the following November, Johnson won reelection. New national lending policies meant that Citizens Trust Bank received increased capital and greater opportunity.

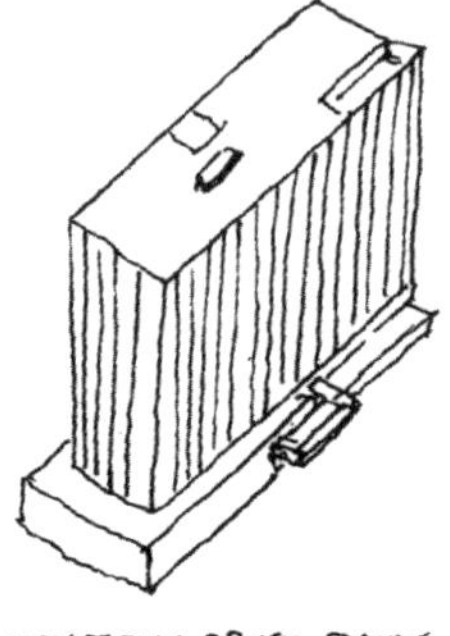

CITIZENS TRUST BANK

In this era of promise and prosperity, Citizens Trust constructed a new headquarters at 75 Piedmont Avenue that served as its home for the next half-century. In 2007, Citizens Trust sold the building to Georgia State University, though the bank continued operating there until 2016, when it relocated to 230 Peachtree Street. The school has maintained the building's name internally and nodded to the bank's legacy by using the structure to house offices involved in accounting, financial planning, budgeting, and risk management as well as an office of the state's Small Business Development Center network.

Although the heart of the business has moved up the street a few blocks, Citizens Trust Bank left plenty of soul behind. On the ground level at 75 Piedmont, you'll find Kenley's Catering and Restaurant, which opened in 2000 at the invitation of the bank's president. There you'll be treated to southern hospitality along with delicious green beans, baked chicken, collards, mac and cheese, and meatloaf and some of the best fried chicken and cornbread muffins Atlanta has to offer. And Kenley Waller himself will greet you with a warm smile that matches those of the many celebrity patrons whose photos grace the walls and contribute to the story of a building with seriously rich history.

# *Atlanta Daily World* Building

**145 AUBURN AVENUE**

Built at a cost of $3,500 in 1912—the same year that saw the founding of the Girl Scouts in Savannah, the opening of Fenway Park in Boston, and statehood for Arizona and New Mexico—the *Atlanta Daily World* Building witnessed numerous upheavals during the twentieth century, including great fires, Prohibition, a tornado, two world wars, and the Great Depression. The newspaper for which the building is named was at one time the longest continuously operating African American daily publication in U.S. history, and both the Daily World and its headquarters played major roles in the Civil Rights Movement.

The building predates the newspaper by a decade and a half. The *Atlanta Daily World* was founded on August 5, 1928, by William Alexander Scott, an entrepreneur who used syndication to grow his enterprise into fifty publications. Scott believed that "the responsibility of a Negro newspaper is to dispense to the public good wholesome information to enlighten our people . . . and to serve as a guide and organ of expression for the community."[1] When the thirty-one-year-old Scott was mysteriously murdered outside his home in 1934, his brother, Cornelius Adolphus Scott took the reins, leading with zeal for nearly six decades. C. A. Scott was later followed by W. A. Scott's granddaughter, former *Atlanta Journal-Constitution* reporter and editor M. Alexis Scott.

Originally located in an Auburn Avenue building owned by Big Bethel Church, the *Atlanta Daily World* bought 145 Auburn Avenue from Mabel Driskell in 1946. Driskell, a Black entrepreneur who owned the Dris-Kura Manufacturing Company, which made hair and beauty products, as well as the Dermis Cura College of Beauty Culture, had bought the building just two years earlier as an investment and never occupied space in it. The newspaper operated out of the building for the next sixty-two years, initially operating on the top level and later expanding to both floors.

Throughout its history, the paper has been not only a strong voice for Black residents of Sweet Auburn and Atlanta but also a platform for progress. Martin Luther King Sr., John Wesley Dobbs, Dr. Martin Luther King Jr., and other leaders of the Civil Rights Movement met in the building to debate, plan, and proselytize for the cause. The paper's impact and news spread beyond the strict confines of the neighborhood. On February 8, 1944, the *Daily World*'s Harry S. Alpin became the first Black reporter to cover the White House. In 1980, the Society of Professional Journalists designated the *Daily World* Building a "Historic Site in Journalism," as the plaque on the building's front facade proclaims.

Before the newspaper moved in, 145 Auburn Avenue served a variety of other entrepreneurial, civic, and social functions. Beginning in 1918, the Virgil Coffee Company brought a buzz to the block, selling beans on the bottom level for 17 years. In the late 1920s and 1930s, white and Black private residences filled the second floor, known as 143½ Auburn Avenue. In 1944, the apartments were replaced by District V, Atlanta's first Black Girl Scout troop, which had been founded by Bazoline Usher four doors down the preceding year.

Girl Scouts founder Juliette Gordon Low had intended the organization to be inclusive of all of America and all of the world, proclaiming in the 1913 *Girl Scout Handbook*, "The work of today is the history of tomorrow, and we are its makers."[2] In 1913, the first integrated troop was formed in Bedford, Massachusetts, with the first all-Black troop following four years later. Despite the organization's Georgia origins, however, Atlanta did not have a Black Girl Scout troop prior to 1943.

The brave women and girls of District V showed what was possible. They worked, played, cared for others, and competed with pride, selling more cookies than all but one other Atlanta troop in their inaugural year. District V also helped set the stage for civil rights successes to come, as members grew into well-prepared difference-makers.

One District V alumna, Roslyn Pope, graduated from Booker T. Washington High School and went on to Spelman College, where she was a senior when she penned "An Appeal for Human Rights," the manifesto that launched the Atlanta Student Movement and its sit-ins against discrimination. Pope's appeal was published with help from other Atlanta University Center student and faculty leaders on March 9, 1960, as a paid advertisement in the *Atlanta Journal*, the *Atlanta Constitution*, and the *Atlanta Daily World* and was later reprinted by the *New York Times*. The publicity helped lead to the April 1960 founding of the Student Nonviolent Coordinating Committee (SNCC) and the national student movement. Many other Scouts worked behind the scenes, making posters and writing and editing speeches to make their mark on civil rights history.

On August 30, 1961, five years after Dr. King recognized the Girl Scouts as "a force for desegregation," District V's Madelyn Nix

became one of the Atlanta Nine, the first Black students to integrate the public school system, when she enrolled at Brown High School.[3]

Despite the gains of the Civil Rights and Women's Rights Movements and the recent focus on diversity, equity, and inclusion, women, especially women of color, still take a back seat to their male counterparts socially, in business, and in recognition of achievement. The story of District V provides an opportunity to change the script, to illuminate another form of preservation, the preservation of rights. In the fall of 2023, a mural honoring Pope and District V was unveiled on the eastern-facing side of the *Daily World* Building. The mural was intended to start conversations and inspire new generations to learn about the history that took place at that location. The Girl Scouts of Greater Atlanta have created a patch to encourage Scouts and their families to travel to the historic district and become part of a new movement that supports and celebrates women's rights and Black history through preservation of place.

While District V was making herstory on the second floor of the *Daily World* Building, an entirely different sort of brigade was taking up residence down below. In 1944, Club Poinciana opened its doors on the ground level with a grand opening hyped by manager Johnnie Johnson in the *Atlanta Daily World*:

> The Management is pleased to announce the opening of the Supper Club, Poinciana, located at 145 Auburn Avenue, N.E., Thursday, October 26, 1944, at the hours of 8 p.m. 'til 4 a.m.
>
> Presenting in person, Helen Humes, vocalist, who sang and made famous such recordings as "Unlucky Woman," "Can't Write, Gonna Buy Myself a Telephone," and "And The Angels Sing," and Atlanta's own Connie Berry, radio, stage, screen, and recording artist, at the piano. This nationally known musical attraction will be presented nightly for your entertainment.[4]

Humes, had who replaced the legendary Billie Holiday in the Count Basie Orchestra during the late 1930s and early 1940s, was a successful and versatile talent whom Basie discovered at Cincinnati's Cotton Club in 1937. Humes initially turned down Basie's thirty-five-dollar-per-week offer, but in March 1938, producer John Hammond helped convince her to accompany the band for the next four years. Of that time, Humes recalled,

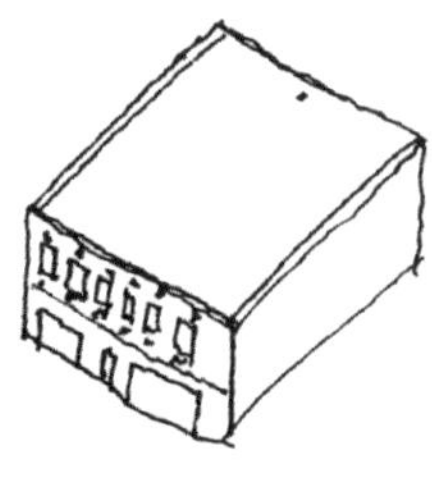

ATLANTA DAILY WORLD

> I used to pretend I was asleep on the Basie bus, . . . so the boys wouldn't think I was hearing their rough talk. I'd sew buttons on and cook for them too. I used to carry pots and a little hot plate around, and I'd fix up some food backstage or in places where it was difficult to get anything to eat when we were down South. Playing cards was the best way of passing time on those long trips, but sometimes when I won money from them I found I had to lend it back! I wasn't interested in drinking and keeping late hours, so that part didn't hurt me. But my kidneys couldn't stand the punishment of those long rides. I was too timid to ask the driver to stop when I should have. Then, too, I got tired of singing the same songs.[5]

Other legends who performed at Club Poinciana included Louis Armstrong, who made a Fourth of July appearance in 1945, Billie Holiday, and Little Richard. In November 1945, Benny Goodman played "hot numbers for the people, lasting late in the morning, until 3 o'clock."[6] The District V Scouts heard the bands as they practiced during the day, the music majestically wafting up and embedding itself into the cultural landscape and into memories.

The *Atlanta Daily World* took over both floors of the building in 1971 and would likely still be there today had Mother Nature not intervened. On March 14, 2008, a tornado tore off the building's roof, exposing the intricate, brick-patterned interior to the elements and resulting in black mold, rotting wood, buckling roof joists, broken glass, and crumbling plaster. For the next four years, 145 Auburn Avenue sat vacant and lifeless.

In March 2012, a developer applied for a demolition permit. More than one thousand civic- and culturally minded petitioners rallied in opposition and asked the Atlanta Urban Design Commission (a Department of City Planning oversight organization focused on preservation) to deny the permit. Their voices were heard, and exactly a century after its construction, a building known almost exclusively for its history could imagine a future.

Cultural developer and preservationist Gene Kansas and his partner, Ben Dupuy, bought the building in 2014. Working with Gamble + Gamble Architects, Dakota Contractors, and other talented architects, engineers, and craftspeople, the owners led a yearlong effort to rehabilitate the building. Its survival serves as a testament to community action and political will. The project garnered numerous awards, including the 2014 "#2 Preservation Win" from the National Trust for Historic Preservation and 2015 honors from the Atlanta Preservation Center, the Georgia Trust for Historic Preservation, and the Atlanta Urban Design Commission.

The *Daily World* Building's grand reopening occurred on March 12, 2015—103 years to the day after the Girl Scouts were founded—with a packed house of community supporters, three members of the Atlanta City Council, and representatives of the National Park Service and the King Center plus preservationists, friends, and longtime residents of Sweet Auburn. Among the sweetest moments was recognition of District V along with several original Girl Scouts, including Celestine Bray Bottoms and Vivienne Brinson. Yes, Thin Mint cookies were served. Ricci de Forest, local celebrity DJ and proprietor of the Madame CJ Walker Museum up the street at the Prince Hall Masonic Lodge, played music by Goodman, Armstrong, and Holiday. People reminisced. It was a great day for Atlanta, setting the tone for the historic building's next chapter.

The *Daily World* Building remains a place for cultural conversation and civic achievement. Today there are two upstairs apartments that are architecturally reminiscent of the 1930s but are occupied by tenants desiring a more modern downtown lifestyle. The lower level features street retail and office space for those looking to have a meaningful connection to and presence in Sweet Auburn.

# 100 Black Men of America

## 141 AUBURN AVENUE

A predominantly white neighborhood during Atlanta's early years, Sweet Auburn's racial demographics began to change after the 1906 Atlanta Massacre led Black residents to congregate and white residents to leave. Within just three years, Auburn Avenue had 117 Black residences and only 74 white. At the same time, an astounding 64 Black businesses were located along the seven-block stretch between Courtland Avenue and Ebenezer Baptist Church.

The two-story white brick building at 141 Auburn Avenue was likely built at least a decade before the neighboring *Atlanta Daily World* Building at 145 Auburn (1912) and the Southern School Book Building at 135 Auburn (1910). A white grocer, James W. Green, occupied the ground level at 141 Auburn for at least ten years, with various tenants renting out the upstairs apartments denoted in the Atlanta City Directory as 141½ Auburn.

Sometime after the neighborhood's demographic transition, the Hopkins Books Concern opened in the building. Said to be Atlanta's first Black bookstore, Hopkins was visited by famed poet, novelist, and activist Langston Hughes in 1947. A print shop later operated at street level before the space became the national home of 100 Black Men of America, which purchased the building in 1997.

Early twentieth century city directories show Auburn Avenue as home to carpenters, streetcar conductors, grocers, salespersons, meat cutters, washerwomen, and porters, more and more of them described

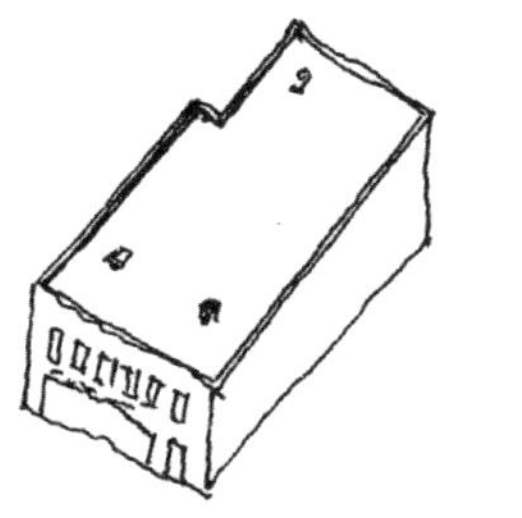

100 BLACK MEN OF AMERICA INC

as colored as the century progressed. These hardworking people registered to vote, participated in marches and sit-ins, worshipped God, and educated their children in Sweet Auburn, building the community that would incubate the Civil Rights Movement.

Many residents who gained recognition as national icons started out as neighborhood activists. John Wesley Dobbs was a railway mail clerk for thirty-two years who led Black voter registration efforts and built the Prince Hall Masonic Lodge, also on Auburn Avenue. Evelyn Gibson, a lifelong civil rights activist, married future Southern Christian Leadership Conference leader Joseph Lowery in 1950 and marched from Selma to Montgomery in 1965. Annie L. Watters McPheeters was a brilliant leader who started the Negro History Collection at Atlanta's first library for African Americans. Alberta Christine Williams married a reverend and became mother to a King. John Robert Lewis was a "boy from Troy" who came from Alabama to follow Martin Luther King Jr. and stir up "good trouble" before speaking at the March on Washington and becoming a beloved U.S. representative for Georgia's Fifth District. It is not surprising that they came from the community—they *made* the community.

As the Civil Rights Movement reached its height in 1963, a group of Black men met in New York City to institutionalize the mentorship of new leaders. They created "the 100" out of care and concern for their communities, hoping to change the future.

These founders were visionary, accomplished, and motivated to give back to their community. They included future New York City mayor David Dinkins; Judge Robert Mangum; surgeon and Bronze Star recipient Dr. William Hayling, who served as the organization's first national president; and his successor, philanthropist and entrepreneur Nathaniel Goldston III.

Other early notable members of 100 Black Men of America included Harlem civic leader and New York State Supreme Court justice

Livingston Wingate; Andrew Hatcher, associate press secretary to President John F. Kennedy and the first Black person to serve in the White House Press Office; and Major League Baseball legend and activist Jackie Robinson.

Over the next two decades, the organization operated in New York City and opened other chapters across the United States. On October 2, 1986, chapter representatives convened in Washington, D.C., to inaugurate a national organization, 100 Black Men of America, that took as its motto, "What They See Is What They'll Be."

On May 27, 1987, the group came to Atlanta for its first national conference. Maynard H. Jackson Jr., John Wesley Dobbs's grandson and Atlanta's first Black mayor, spoke to the attendees, signaling the power of generational leadership. Nearly forty years later, the vision that began with just 100 men has now provided a beacon of leadership to 125,000 mentees around the world. The organization owes its extraordinary impact to the everyday and exceptional teachers, business executives, lawyers, and others who have stepped up and given generously of their time and talent.

This legacy continues at 141 Auburn Avenue, now named the Thomas W. Dortch Jr. Center in honor of the group's former CEO who died in 2023, leaving behind a rich civic and community-driven inheritance. Beloved and admired, Dortch was inspired by his predecessor, fellow entrepreneur Nate Goldston, who personally financed programs and oversaw the organization's expansion from fourteen to forty chapters. With Dortch at the helm, 100 Black Men of America topped one hundred chapters and became a global organization with outposts in the Bahamas, England, Senegal, and beyond. Its success stands as another example of how intentional leadership reverberates from one generation to another in Sweet Auburn.

THE THOMAS W.
100 BLACK MEN OF AMERICA INC
141 AUBURN AVE NE

# Atlanta Life Insurance Company

**BUILDING AND ANNEX**
**142-148 AUBURN AVENUE**

Founded over a century ago by Alonzo F. Herndon, a formerly enslaved man who became America's first Black millionaire, the Atlanta Life Insurance Company remains in operation and is now the second-largest Black insurance company in the United States as well as its oldest majority-Black-owned financial institution.

The Auburn Avenue building where Atlanta Life prospered for more than six decades has been less resilient in recent years. The neoclassical Atlanta Life Insurance Company Building was built before 1892, with the facade and Annex added in 1927. It represents what may be one of Atlanta's most underappreciated historical landmarks, but it now stands vacant, with noticeable cracks. Atlanta Life occupied the site from 1920 to 1980, when it moved next door to 100 Auburn Avenue. Georgia State University bought that building in 2013 and renamed it Centennial Hall in honor of the university's one hundredth anniversary. Atlanta Life now has a Peachtree Street address.

Alonzo Franklin Herndon was born on June 26, 1858, in Walton County, Georgia. His father was a white enslaver, Frank Herndon; his mother, Sophenie, was an enslaved woman. At the end of the Civil War, seven-year-old Alonzo and his mother became sharecroppers in Social Circle, Georgia, approximately forty miles outside of Atlanta. In 1878, with only one year of formal education and a mere eleven dollars to his name, Alonzo moved to Coweta County and apprenticed with a barber. Five years later, he landed in

Atlanta and put his sharp business acumen to use as he began his entrepreneurial career. Herndon founded the Crystal Palace and two other high-end barbershops that catered to white clients, providing him with status and financial stability. Located at 66 Peachtree Street, the European-inspired Crystal Palace was opulent, but it also bore witness to one of Atlanta's earliest and most horrific moments in the international spotlight: the Atlanta Massacre of 1906. During widespread riots, white mobs attacked Black citizens and businesses, killing at least twenty people, among them the owners of a Black barbershop across the street from the Crystal Palace. Herndon had closed his shop early that day and was not present for the massacre, but the business's windows were broken, and he closed it permanently later that year.

Herndon had already begun amassing funds from his barbershops and from savvy real estate investing and using the money to acquire benevolent societies and mutual aid associations operated by Black churches. These sophisticated financial support groups served as precursors to Black-owned insurance companies like Atlanta Life. Georgia's stringent capital requirements for insurance businesses forced the Black community to rely heavily on charity in times of crisis. Herndon aggregated the benevolent societies into the Atlanta Mutual Insurance Association and in 1922 incorporated the Atlanta Life Insurance Company, achieving secure legal reserve status, a designation held by only five African American insurance companies at the time.

Herndon was also deeply committed to civil rights and was among the twenty-nine organizing delegates of the 1905 Niagara Movement in Fort Erie, Ontario, which resulted in the formation of the NAACP. Led by W. E. B. Du Bois, the NAACP became the premier national organization providing advocacy and leadership for a range of civil and human rights issues.

On October 31, 1893, Alonzo Herndon married Adrienne McNeil from Augusta, Georgia, who had previously pursued a theatrical career, taking classes in Savannah and at the Boston School of Expression and at the American Academy of Dramatic Arts in New York. With support from Du Bois and other civic-minded leaders, Adrienne Herndon introduced professional theater production to Atlanta University. The Herndons also brought leaders into their home, which Adrienne designed and which was planned and built exclusively by Black architects and tradesmen. The residence is now the Herndon Home Museum, a National Historic Landmark in Atlanta's Westside, but at the turn of the twentieth century, it not only provided a loving environment for the couple's only son, Norris, but also welcomed in a community desirous for entertainment, inspiration, and association until Adrienne's 1910 death.

In May 1912, Alonzo married Jessie Gillespie. Like Adrienne, Jessie Herndon hosted guests at home for social and business purposes and was active in the community, working to benefit the Phyllis Wheatley YWCA and the Gate City Free Kindergarten Association, which operated the Herndon Day Nursery. Jessie Herndon and the wives of other influential businessmen were members of the Twelve Club, and she joined Atlanta Life's board of directors in 1927, appointed by her husband shortly before his death on July 21. She ultimately served as the company's first female vice president prior to her death in 1947.

Alonzo's only child, Norris B. Herndon, was born on July 15, 1897. Norris accompanied his father during the formation of the Niagara Movement, appearing in a photo commemorating the moment. Father and son enjoyed an unbreakable and loving bond, with Norris dedicating himself to advancing his father's achievements. In 1921, Norris earned a master's degree from the Harvard University Business School, and he assumed the presidency of Atlanta Life following his father's death.

Norris not only led the company to new heights but established the Alonzo F. and Norris B. Herndon Foundation, which proved invaluable to the Civil Rights Movement. Norris himself played a pivotal role in the movement's success by materially supporting its leaders and activists.

Adrienne, Jessie, Norris and Alonzo Herndon are all buried at Atlanta's South-View Cemetery, where Alonzo's headstone describes him simply as "a devoted husband and loving father."

# Southern School Book Building

## 135 AUBURN AVENUE

From the beginning, books, knowledge, and enlightenment have been baked into the foundations of 135 Auburn Avenue, known originally as the Southern School Book Building. Constructed in 1910 under the aegis of design firm Hentz & Reid, the structure stands as a stunning example of early twentieth century architecture. Known in the Southeast for their Beaux-Arts style and as the founding fathers of the Georgia school of classicism, Hentz & Reid designed many of Atlanta's homes and commercial buildings, including another influential Sweet Auburn landmark, the Butler Street YMCA.

Neel Reid, who joined Hal Hentz in 1909, hand-drew a set of spectacular and symmetrical plans for a warehouse that would sell books wholesale to school systems around the region. Reid's design set an intellectual tone from the street level up by featuring ornate garland swags across the top of the pediment, which is capped by a majestic seal centered with the torch of knowledge and an open book.

The Southern School Book Building was not just about books, however; it was also about knowledge and action. Sweet Auburn forefather John Wesley Dobbs often proclaimed that "bucks, ballots, and books" were the key ingredients to true freedom. Decades after the building's construction, the student activists of the Civil Rights Movement rallied these elements together through publishing, voter registration, and fundraising and by banding together to help realize a shared vision.

John Lewis had an office at 135 Auburn Avenue while chairing the Student Nonviolent Coordinating Committee (SNCC) in 1963, the same year fellow activist Medgar Evers was murdered and the movement organized the March on Washington. SNCC staff member Julian Bond also spent time at 135 Auburn Avenue as communications director and editor of the organization's weekly newspaper, the *Student Voice*. It has also been rumored that the Freedom Riders of the early 1960s slept in the building, which seems plausible given the operational support SNCC provided to those efforts. The building thus was a central meeting place for leaders and practitioners of direct action and nonviolence, the fundamental strategies laid out by movement leaders Martin Luther King Jr., Ella Baker, Diane Nash, James Bevel, Andrew Young, and others.

After passage of the Civil Rights Act of 1964 and King's assassination in 1968, Sweet Auburn receded as a hotbed of activism. During the white flight era of the 1970s, the neighborhood fell into disrepair, and the warehouse at 135 Auburn Avenue went from selling books to selling tires. In 1978, however, the APEX Museum, Atlanta's oldest Black history museum, dedicated to exploring what it calls the "African-American Panoramic Experience," was founded by Dan Moore Sr., who renovated the building in 1985 with help from E. R. Mitchell Construction.

For nearly forty years starting in the 1980s, the Southern Education Foundation (SEF) occupied the top level, while APEX operated below. The foundation traces its roots back to 1867, when the $1 million Peabody Education Fund was organized. Peabody placed few restrictions on its funds other than requiring that they be used to uplift the poorest communities of the U.S. South and Southwest through education, with a particular focus on teacher training and recruitment.

In 1937, the Peabody Fund and several like-minded organizations, among them the Jeanes and Slater Funds, consolidated to form the SEF, initially located in Washington, D.C. The foundation moved to Atlanta in 1947, first opening offices on Spring Street before moving into the historic district and onto Auburn Avenue in the 1980s.

The foundation's forerunner organizations supported W. E. B. Du Bois as their first fellow in 1903, the same year he published *The Souls of Black Folk*. These organizations were also instrumental in supporting historically Black colleges as they navigated desegregation and accreditation.

Leaders who served from this historic address include Elridge McMillan, a thirty-four-year member of the University System of Georgia's Board of Regents and its first African American chair, who joined the SEF in 1968 and became its first Black leader as well prior to his 2001 retirement; Lynn Walker Huntley, who served as the foundation's first female president (2002–10); and Dr. Cyril Kent McGuire, SEF president from 2010 to 2017. Raymond C. Pierce became the organization's president and CEO in 2018, shortly after it decided to move to new offices on Marietta Street near Centennial Olympic Park.

In April 2017, Gene Kansas and other impact-investment partners bought the former SEF space and began to reimagine the top level of the building. The ambitious and imaginative revitalization plan culminated in Constellations, a civic, social, and cultural workspace

SOUTHERN SCHOOL BOOK BUILDING

135 AUBURN AVE NE

that brings together people focused on improving society. Constellations cultivates an ecosystem that honors the world-renowned history of Sweet Auburn while providing a relaxed professional environment in which purpose-driven companies, historians, writers, students, educators, designers, and other cultural talents can live their dreams and fulfill their missions.

Offering private offices and studies, meeting and event opportunities, community gathering spaces, and the Fifth District Studio for the creation of original content and the recording of oral histories, Constellations demonstrates how the Sweet Auburn community continues to attract organizations and people who make a positive difference in the world. The studio's name is an homage to the congressional district John Lewis served for more than three decades.

Since its inception, Constellations has hosted more than five hundred culturally oriented meetings and events such as jazz nights, author talks, panel discussions, company off-sites, theatrical performances, and weddings. The company has contributed more than $150,000 in the form of free office and meeting space and has sponsored an additional $75,000 in programs benefiting community-oriented companies, individuals, and nonprofit corporations.

In 2004, the SEF received a Development of Excellence award from the Atlanta Urban Design Commission for the complete restoration of the building's facade; the commission also bestowed a second award in 2009 for the building's renovation following damage caused by the March 2008 tornado that ripped through downtown Atlanta. Most recently, the commission honored Gene Kansas | Commercial Real Estate and the building with a 2018 Award of Excellence for Historic Preservation for the front facade and the reimagined Constellations space. Gene Kansas | Commercial

Real Estate and Constellations also received Development of Excellence awards from the Atlanta Regional Commission in 2018 and the Urban Land Institute in 2019.

Immediate neighbors to the building include the Auburn Avenue Research Library on African American Culture and History; Georgia State University's Centennial Hall; the *Atlanta Daily World* Building at 145 Auburn; and 141 Auburn Avenue, currently the national headquarters of 100 Black Men of America and once the city's first African American bookstore. This stretch of Auburn Avenue represents a Block of Knowledge, illuminating the neighborhood's history and continuing to honor the district's heritage of fostering civic identity and activism through education.

Conveniently located on the Atlanta Streetcar line and surrounded by Georgia State University buildings, the Southern School Book Building is just a short walk from cultural attractions, historic sites, and some of the district's favorite treats, including the delicious desserts at Sweet Auburn Bread Company and the phenomenal baked chicken, green beans, and cornbread at Kenley's.

SOUTHERN SCHOOL BOOK BUILDING

# Centennial Hall

**GEORGIA STATE UNIVERSITY**
**100 AUBURN AVENUE**

The building now known as Centennial Hall opened in 1980, ushering one of Sweet Auburn's oldest Black businesses into a more modern era. The six-story, 105,000-square-foot office building was originally constructed to house the Atlanta Life Insurance Company, founded by Alonzo Franklin Herndon, a formerly enslaved person, sharecropper, barber, and iconic entrepreneur. The company had already operated for more than six decades at 142-148 Auburn Avenue before moving into Herndon Plaza next door at 100 Auburn. The building was designed by Joseph Robinson, one of the first three Black architects to establish a firm in Georgia. In 1995, at age sixty-eight, Robinson became the state's first Black Fellow in the American Institute of Architects.

Though Robinson received a bachelor's degree in architecture from Hampton Institute, discrimination meant that he could not find employment in the field, and he first worked as a teacher, spending fifteen years at Booker T. Washington High School. He instilled in his students a deep appreciation for Black contributions to American design. While teaching, he worked as a residential architect, designing more than two hundred houses, and in 1970, he founded J. W. Robinson & Associates; the firm played a foundational role in preserving Sweet Auburn and establishing the Martin Luther King Jr. National Historical Park. The firm carried out renovations of such iconic structures as the King Birth Home, the Odd Fellows Building, and Ebenezer Baptist Church, to name a few.

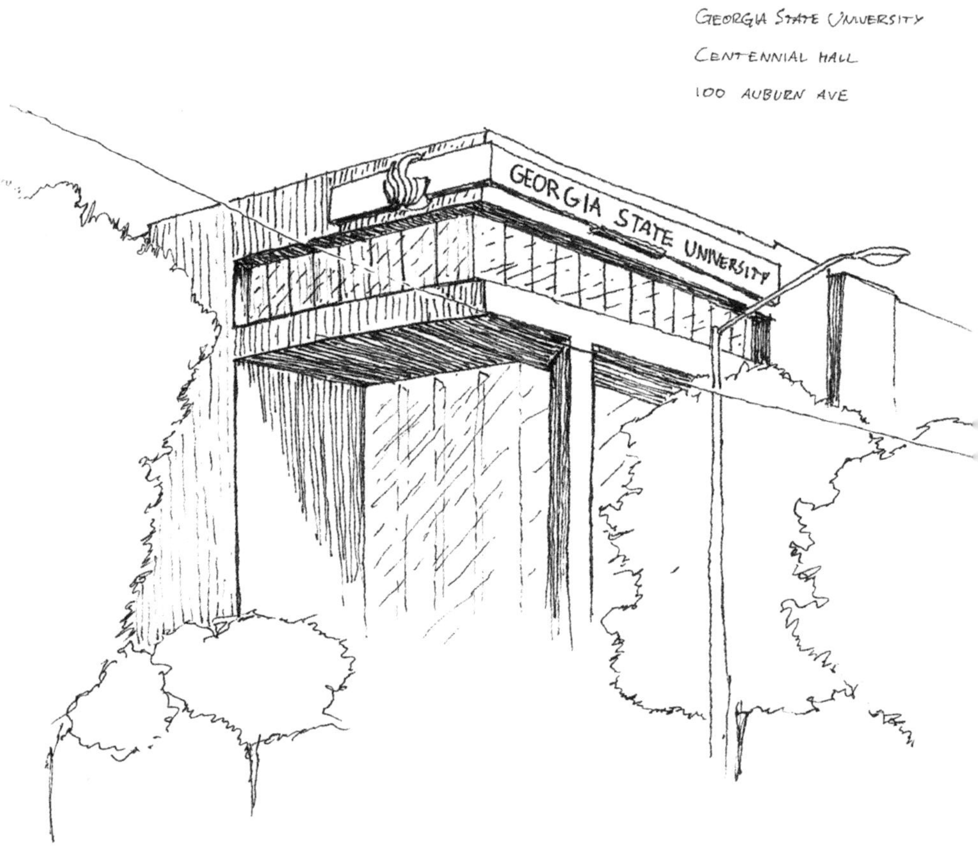

Atlanta Life's roots go back to 1905, when Herndon invested $140 to acquire the Atlanta Benevolent and Protective Association, which had been organized by the Reverend Peter James Bryant of Wheat Street Baptist Church. Such benevolent societies took the place of insurance companies within the Black community, and Herndon acquired several others as well as insurance firms and protective unions, bundling them under the banner of Atlanta Mutual Insurance Association. By 1922, the company's assets topped $400,000 (about $5.6 million today), and Herndon consolidated the company as Atlanta Life.

Herndon went on to become Atlanta's wealthiest Black citizen and the country's first Black millionaire, leveraging his fortune and connections to advance causes tied to Black advancement and preserve Black-owned businesses. His son, Norris B. Herndon, who received an MBA from Harvard University in 1921, followed in his father's footsteps, becoming an anonymous funder of the Civil Rights Movement.

In 2013, Georgia State University acquired 100 Auburn Avenue from Atlanta Life, which moved its offices to 191 Peachtree Street, where the company still operates today. Georgia State renovated the building and renamed it Centennial Hall in honor of the school's one hundredth anniversary. It now houses the GSU Welcome Center as well as offices for the Honors College, alumni relations, the president, and the provost. The clean-lined stone-and-glass building also includes meeting space and a 246-seat auditorium jutting out toward Auburn Avenue on the ground level.

Expanding Georgia State's presence in Sweet Auburn was fitting, given the street's pivotal role in driving educational attainment for Atlanta's Black community. GSU is now Georgia's largest university by enrollment, with a diverse majority-minority student population of approximately 54,000. Some 33,000 students attend classes at the ever-growing main campus downtown, with the remainder attending the school's other Atlanta-area campuses. GSU has been instrumental in the revitalization of downtown Atlanta and contributes nearly $2.8 billion annually to the state's economy.

Georgia State integrated in 1962, a year after the University of Georgia and Georgia Tech. Annette Lucille Hall, a social studies teacher, became the first Black student, enrolling in a required continuing education class, the Institute on Americanism and Communism.

One of Georgia State's most prestigious schools carries the name of civil rights icon Andrew Young, a former Atlanta mayor and U.S. ambassador to the United Nations. Located on campus just a few blocks away from Centennial Hall, the Andrew Young School of Policy Studies is a model for inclusivity in higher education. Nearly 20 percent of its graduate students in economics, public policy, and other disciplines come from developing countries; 59 percent are women, and about half are Black.

Young was a close confidant of Martin Luther King Jr. and was with him when he was assassinated in Memphis, Tennessee, in 1968. As the Southern Christian Leadership Conference's executive director, Young became an integral leader and strategist in the Civil Rights Movement before launching his diplomatic and political career. Even into his nineties, Young has remained active in Atlanta, lending a respected voice of conscience to the contemporary fight for justice and equality.

In addition to the Andrew Young School, Georgia State University is also home to a second impressive institution bearing the name of another Atlanta trailblazer, Herman J. Russell Sr., founder of H. J. Russell & Company and the first Black member of the Atlanta Chamber of Commerce. Russell earned a degree in building construction from Tuskegee Institute in 1952 and later that year founded an Atlanta plastering business that grew into Russell & Company, one of the most successful Black-owned real estate and construction companies in the United States. According to its tagline, the H. J. Russell Center for Entrepreneurship seeks "to empower a new generation of passionate leaders." The center hosts talks by influential speakers and authors as well as by hosting a business model competition.

On the other side of downtown, the Russell Innovation Center for Entrepreneurs (RICE) is located in Russell & Company's former headquarters in Castleberry Hill. The fifty-four-thousand-square-foot building underwent a transformative renovation in 2016, and the organization is supported by many hometown favorites, including the Atlanta Hawks. By virtue of his stake in the Omni Group, Russell also owned a portion of the Hawks, making him the first Black person in the United States to have a shareholder interest in a major professional sports team.

In Atlanta, Russell's company has constructed many skyline-enhancing buildings, including the former Georgia Dome, Mercedes Benz Stadium, the National Center for Civil and Human Rights, and Hartsfield International Airport (now Hartsfield-Jackson).The company also helped with Atlanta's Olympic transformation. In addition, Russell was a central figure in the Civil Rights Movement, providing both guidance and financing. His home served as a meeting place for Martin Luther King Jr., Ralph David Abernathy, John Lewis, Andrew Young, and other leaders during the 1960s.

Russell died in 2014 and is buried in South-View Cemetery, as are other influential Black entrepreneurs and leaders such as Alonzo F. Herndon, Carrie "Mama" Cunningham, John Wesley Dobbs, Julian Bond, and Benjamin E. Mays. Today, Russell's sons, H. Jerome Russell Jr. and Michael Russell Sr., and daughter, Donata Russell Ross, are keeping the family businesses and the spirit of entrepreneurship alive and well in the city they love.

# Auburn Avenue Research Library on African American Culture and History

## 101 AUBURN AVENUE

The Auburn Avenue Research Library on African American Culture and History is a celebrated and unique institution. Part of the Fulton County public library system, the Auburn Avenue Research Library possesses a trove of archival material preserving the legacies and accomplishments of African-descended people in the United States. Beyond its obvious importance as a repository, the library also offers vibrant community-based programming in the arts, literature, and education.

But before the library carved out this cultural niche and took up residence at its current corner in the Sweet Auburn district, it began down the street as the Auburn Branch of the Carnegie Library of Atlanta, the city's first public library for African Americans. In the early 1880s, steel magnate Andrew Carnegie had begun funding the construction of public libraries across the country, and the effort took off around the turn of the twentieth century. In the South, Carnegie followed Jim Crow, constructing separate libraries for African Americans.

The first of three African American branches of the Atlanta–Fulton County Public Library System opened on July 25, 1921. Located at 333 Auburn Avenue, the original branch operated under the direction of longtime educator Alice Dugged Cary, who served as librarian until 1929. Beginning in 1934, the library housed the Negro History Collection of Non-Circulating Books, which

consisted of scholarly journals, bound magazines, and newspapers for and about Black residents, including Sweet Auburn's *Atlanta Daily World*. In 1936, Annie L. Watters McPheeters, the library's first professional librarian, began her thirty-year tenure, during which time the branch became a nexus in the community.

On December 6, 1949, the West Hunter Branch (now the Washington Park Library) opened on Atlanta's west side to serve the growing Black community there, and the Negro History Collection was moved to the new branch. The original Auburn Avenue library closed in 1959, the same year the Atlanta–Fulton County Public Library System was officially integrated, though Black patrons were permitted only to read in the basements of the previously white-only libraries and could not check out books. On May 19, 1959, Irene Dobbs Jackson, the eldest daughter of John Wesley Dobbs, became the first Black person to receive a card that allowed her access to the main branches of the Atlanta Public Library, integrating the system and paving the way for both greater literacy and greater equality. Her son, Maynard Jackson Jr., later became Atlanta's first Black mayor.

In 1970, during a new era of integration, the Negro History Collection was moved once again, this time to the downtown Carnegie Library (now the site of the Fulton County Central Library). In 1971, the library system's board of trustees officially named the collection in honor of Samuel W. Williams, a civil rights leader and former senior pastor of Friendship Baptist Church who had been a mentor and teacher of Maynard Jackson Jr., Martin Luther King Jr., and Samuel DuBois Cook, who went on to become president of Dillard University in New Orleans.

In 1980, the original Carnegie Library was replaced by the Central Library (the last building designed by Bauhaus architect Marcel Breuer). The Samuel W. Williams Collection on Black America remained there until 1994, when it was moved to the new Auburn Avenue Research Library at 101 Auburn Avenue. In 2014, the library closed and underwent a $20 million renovation, reopening on August 4, 2016, with the Williams Collection anchoring the Reference and Research Division. Patrons can access a variety of textual and microform records, a noncirculating library of secondary sources, and a broad array of digital research databases for the study of African American and African diaspora culture and history.

To bring life to the library's collections, the Programs Division organizes and hosts readings, exhibitions, film screenings, lectures, seminars, tours, and workshops. These activities happen on the building's main level, which features an auditorium, an education center, and two exhibition spaces, including the Cary-McPheeters Gallery.

VIEW FROM IN FRONT OF RESEARCH LIBRARY
101 AUBURN AVE

## AN OVERVIEW

*Through food, drink, and programming, the sights in this chapter whet the appetite for preserving place and showcase how leadership, determination, and dedication to a cause can make a meaningful difference.*

*This chapter shares a segment of the story that falls a bit outside the boundaries of the earlier chapters. Some of the spaces, places, and characters highlighted here lie outside the borders of Sweet Auburn proper but offer context for the neighborhood and make history in newly imagined and sometimes unconventional ways. Their stories are colorful, tasty, refreshing, and motivating.*

*Enjoy!*

CHAPTER 5

# EDGEWOOD AND DOWNTOWN

*Food, Drink, and Historymaking Moments*

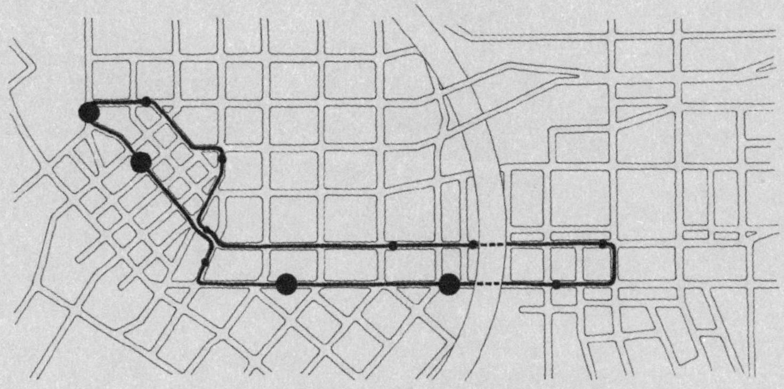

ATLANTA STREETCAR STOPS: MULTIPLE
WEST TO EAST: CENTENNIAL OLYMPIC PARK, LUCKIE AT CONE, HURT PARK, SWEET AUBURN MARKET

**THE CURB MARKET**
209 EDGEWOOD AVENUE

**DIXIE COCA-COLA BOTTLING COMPANY PLANT**
125 EDGEWOOD AVENUE

**HERREN'S**
84 LUCKIE STREET

**NATIONAL CENTER FOR CIVIL AND HUMAN RIGHTS**
CENTENNIAL OLYMPIC PARK

CURB STREET MARKET
209 EDGEWOOD AVE SE

# The Curb Market

## 209 EDGEWOOD AVENUE

The Great Fire of 1917 left much of Atlanta's Old Fourth Ward desolate, carving a mile-long path of destruction through the heart of the city. The fire displaced thousands of people, especially among the Black community. To sow new seeds of commerce and opportunity, an improvised open-air market operated from 1918 to 1923 in what is now the Sweet Auburn National Historic Landmark District, which includes the Martin Luther King Jr. National Historical Park as well as other sites in the Sweet Auburn neighborhood.The marketplace's success led to calls for a permanent "fireproof" structure, and the Women's Club of Atlanta raised money to bring it to fruition.

The Municipal Market of Atlanta opened on May 1, 1924, selling meat and farm-fresh produce directly to consumers.The market was ostensibly meant for people of all classes and colors, but in the Jim Crow South, commerce was inherently inequitable. Black vendors couldn't sell within the market halls but instead were relegated to carts outside, leading to the name by which it is known today: the Curb Market.

The brick-and-concrete building was designed by A. Ten Eyck Brown, a prominent Atlanta architect who made his name working on public buildings. In addition to monumental courthouses around the South, Brown is known for landmarks such as the Fulton County Courthouse and the Martin Luther King Jr. Federal

Building, both of which are listed on the National Register of Historic Places. He also devised the 1925 classical design for Atlanta City Hall, which was rejected but became the foundational plan for the majestic twenty-eight-floor Dade County Courthouse in Miami, Florida. It was completed in 1928, the tallest building in that city at the time.

The Atlanta Municipal Market's footprint is triangular, following the form of the surrounding city blocks. Smaller in stature than Brown's other public edifices, the attractive yet utilitarian market stands 1.5 stories high, with arched brick towers at each end flanking expansive open bays for deliveries and merchandising. The interior features an open design, offering flexibility and a historical nod to the large tent where the market initially operated.

Perhaps ironically for a market that started with a strict local focus and a complex history fraught with exclusion, the Curb Market is commonly lauded today for its culinary diversity. Much like the city it represents, the market offers a chance to experience new flavors and ideas and provides a gathering spot for people from all walks of life—longtime neighborhood residents who have shopped there since MLK Jr. preached around the corner; Georgia State University students exploring downtown for the first time; doctors and nurses at Grady and Children's Hospitals; tourists visiting the birthplace of the Civil Rights Movement. The Curb Market attracts everyone.

The market's survival was not always assured. As shopping habits shifted toward supermarkets and the surrounding area declined, the Curb Market's prospects dimmed. It was threatened with closure on multiple occasions, but every time, its contribution to Atlanta's commercial history and its utility as a place for specialty produce and cultural variety won out, prompting infusions of public and private funds. While patrons can still find cow hooves, butchered hogs, seafood, chicken feet, and fresh produce, today's Curb Market boasts more eateries than market stalls. But it still delivers astounding diversity, as pressed juices, candied pralines, and gelato intermingle with soul food and old-school voodoo ingredients, a unique mix in Atlanta—or anywhere.

The 2014 creation of the Atlanta Streetcar, which includes a stop right outside the market's Edgewood Avenue front door, was touted as having the potential to transform the area along the 2.7-mile route between the King Center and Centennial Olympic Park. Proponents claimed that the infrastructure investment would encourage development. To date, the results have been mixed, but the Curb Market seems to be drawing its share of riders who want to enjoy lunch in an enduring landmark.

Hungry for history and a bite? Rawesome Juicery is great for cold-pressed juices, Miss D's Pralines will set you free, Afrodish serves up delicious hot curry chicken, and Metro Deli Soul Food is the spot for breakfast, beet salad, or baked chicken. On the hearty side, try Panbury's Double Crust Pies for a delicious déjeuner, and don't miss out on La Vegano, a friendly spot for those interested in vegan options. Then top it off with the Italian-inspired delights at Three Peaches Gelato & Coffee.

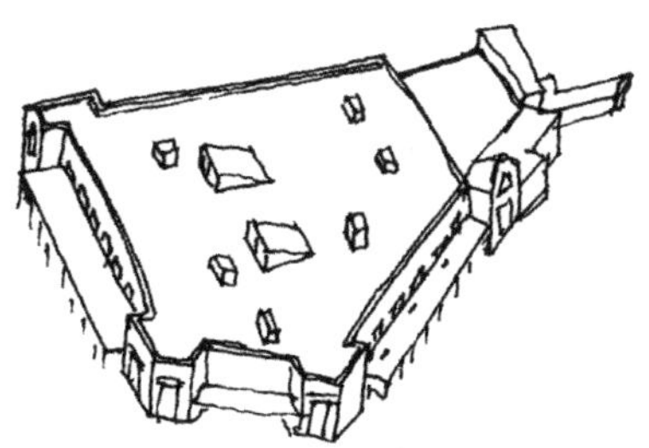

CURB MARKET

MUNICIPAL MARKET
209 EDGEWOOD AVE SE

# Dixie Coca-Cola Bottling Company Plant

## 125 EDGEWOOD AVENUE

The Coca-Cola formula was invented by pharmacist John Pemberton in 1886. Pemberton's syrup, when blended with carbonated water, created what the company labeled a "Delicious and Refreshing" combination. The drink was first served at Jacobs' Pharmacy, near what is today the corner of Marietta and Peachtree Streets. The product soon saw a fizzy acceleration in demand, both at drugstore soda fountains and in bottled form.

Bottling plants today conjure images of sleek, sterile production lines, but the Dixie Coca-Cola Bottling Company Plant in Sweet Auburn shows that such was not always the case. Built in 1891, the Victorian building at the corner of Courtland Street and Edgewood Avenue evokes a San Francisco style, an unconventional architectural motif for a factory that still stands out on the block today. The Dutch stepped gable with an oval window, Italian Renaissance–inspired arcade, square turret, round-arched windows, and pyramidal hipped roof combine to lend a European feel to a building now surrounded by Georgia State fraternity houses and towering student housing developments.

Originally configured with street-level shops topped by living space, the building was filled with entrepreneurs bottling up their new concoction in the basement's automated factory while managers sat in offices above. The Dixie Coca-Cola Bottling Company, parent of the

DIXIE COCA-COLA BOTTLING COMPANY PLANT
125 EDGEWOOD AVE

Coca-Cola Bottling Company, had its headquarters here for about a year starting in 1900 until exponential growth necessitated a move.

In addition to complementing burgers and fries, Coca-Cola pairs well with Atlanta's history as the City Too Busy to Hate. In 1888, shortly before his death, Pemberton sold his interest in Coca-Cola to Asa G. Candler, a savvy Atlanta businessman who led the company to soaring heights. His successor, Robert Winship Woodruff, whose father, Ernest, had bought the company from Candler in 1919 for $25 million ($554.8 million in today's dollars), helped move Atlanta forward and brought together white and Black communities in times of success and sorrow.

Robert Woodruff served as president of the Coca-Cola Company from 1923 until 1955, building incredible wealth and expanding to international markets as the United States fought two world wars. Woodruff remained on the company's board of directors until 1984, maintaining influence not only on Coca-Cola but on the world stage. Woodruff played a pivotal role in encouraging white business owners to buy tickets to a dinner in honor of Martin Luther King Jr.'s 1964 Nobel Peace Prize.

When King was assassinated at the Lorraine Motel in Memphis by James Earl Ray on April 4, 1968, Woodruff and former Georgia governor Carl Sanders received the news while meeting in the Oval Office with President Lyndon Johnson. Woodruff made sure that Atlanta mayor Ivan Allen Jr. and King's widow, Coretta Scott King, knew that they had the company's full support, reportedly telling them that whatever was needed for the funeral, for the family, and to keep the peace in Atlanta would be taken care of.

News of King's death sparked riots in more than one hundred cities, among them New York, Boston, Chicago, Minneapolis, Baltimore, and Winston-Salem, North Carolina. Some fifty-seven thousand National Guard troops were mobilized across the country. Georgia governor Lester Maddox barricaded himself inside the State Capitol, telling the 160 state troopers guarding the grounds that if any protesters tried to make their way inside, the officers should "shoot them down and stack them up."[1] However, thoughtful leadership in the Black community and strategic resistance to violence in the white community enabled Atlanta to remain largely peaceful.

Despite the anxiety, anger, and sadness that accompanied King's death, the Atlanta business community thrived during Mayor Allen's administration (1962–70). In an otherwise tumultuous decade, Atlanta benefited from reform through pragmatic leadership.

Earlier in his career, Allen had been a steadfast segregationist, but he recognized the need for a change of course. He shared Woodruff's belief that turmoil would harm Atlanta and eventually became an advocate for racial equality, as he demonstrated by removing the "Colored" and "White" signs at City Hall on his first day in office. The following year, he publicly supported President John F. Kennedy's efforts to end segregation, becoming the only southern elected official to testify in favor of Kennedy's proposed civil rights bill, which was ultimately passed as the Civil Rights Act of 1964 after the president's murder. In 1981, Coretta Scott King awarded Allen the Martin Luther King Jr. Nonviolent Peace Prize.

After the Dixie Coca-Cola Bottling Company moved out of 125 Edgewood, the building saw multiple uses—a dry goods store, a flag and bunting business, pharmacies, a plumbing and heating company, a shop selling and servicing radios. In 1966, the Atlanta Baptist Association bought the building, and it reopened three years later as Georgia State University's Baptist Student Union, a role it continues today. In 1983, 125 Edgewood was designated a National Historic Landmark.

# Herren's

## 84 LUCKIE STREET

In 1963, with the Civil Rights Movement gathering momentum, Atlanta mayor Ivan Allen Jr. hosted closed-door meetings with white civic leaders and restaurateurs to discuss how the city could end segregation without substantial business upheaval. Given his reputation for pragmatism, the mayor emphasized the prospect of voluntary integration to avoid compelling establishments to open to Black patrons. More than fifty restaurant owners who attended the meetings agreed to allow Black diners, but few of the establishments followed through.

By the early 1960s, Ye Olde Herren's had established itself as a staple of the Atlanta dining scene and was poised for even more rapid growth. Famous for its prominent one-hundred-gallon lobster tank, Herren's doubled its capacity to three hundred seats in 1963, split evenly between upstairs and downstairs dining rooms. Success had not happened overnight; Herren's immigrant founders had endured a forty-year odyssey spanning multiple continents to create what became known as the Restaurant of the Elite for downtown office workers and shoppers.

The story began in Europe. As World War I intensified, Guido Negri took a job on the Hamburg-America Line as a ship's cook, crossing the Atlantic in search of a new life. After a stint as a chef at New York's Biltmore Hotel, Negri moved to Atlanta and cultivated the food and beverage program for a new Biltmore property developed by William Candler, son of Coca-Cola founder Asa Candler, who also served as Atlanta's forty-first mayor. The Atlanta Biltmore elevated Negri's status and allowed him to hone his craft, and not long after its opening on April 19, 1924, he was hired away to accommodate well-heeled diners at the posh Piedmont Driving Club. There, Negri continued to gain experience in hospitality, but he also encountered racial discrimination that foreshadowed his family's revolutionary legacy in the restaurant business.

In 1934, during the Great Depression, prizefighter Charlie "Red" Herren opened the doors of Ye Olde Herren's at Five Points downtown. That year, Adolf Hitler declared himself führer of Germany and fascist Benito Mussolini was elected for the third time in Italy. Mussolini invaded Ethiopia in 1935 before aligning with Germany and Japan to form the Axis Powers leading up to World War II. Anti-Italian sentiment rose in the United States, and Negri's ethnicity led to increased personal discrimination. He would soon leave the Piedmont Driving Club.

Carling Dinkler, head of the Dinkler Hotel chain, which owned the Hotel Ansley on Williams Street in downtown Atlanta, hired Negri and sent him to study operations at New Orleans's luxurious St. Charles Hotel. The Hotel Ansley was renamed the Dinkler Plaza Hotel in 1953 and hosted a 1964 dinner honoring Martin Luther King Jr.'s Nobel Peace Prize that constituted the first integrated formal dinner in Atlanta's history. King and Allen dined together at the head table, enjoying a program that included music by the Morehouse College choir.

In 1939, Negri purchased Herren's from its namesake, keeping the name but moving the establishment from the modest space in

HERREN'S
84 LUCKIE ST NW
THEATRICAL OUTFIT

Five Points to a handsome 18,300-square-foot building at 84 Luckie Street in what is now downtown's Fairlie-Poplar Historic District. A supporter of various community causes, Negri helped to establish the Atlanta Philharmonic Orchestra prior to his death in 1942.

Guido Negri's widow, Amalia, took over Herren's, operating it until 1947, when their son Edward officially took over. Dinner favorites included whole live Maine lobster sold by the pound, Alaskan king crab for $3.00, bacon-wrapped filet mignon, and jumbo shrimp a l'Arnaud—a bite-sized nod to Arnaud Cazenave and the splendid New Orleans restaurant he founded in 1918—for $1.65. Lunch featured southern cuisine for as many as five hundred customers per day. Day or night, dessert included what was billed as the "world's best lemon ice box pie," made with buttered graham cracker crust, and crowd-favorite cinnamon rolls made from scratch daily in the downstairs bakery.

Ed Negri sought to follow in his father's footsteps as a business and civic leader, and in 1963, bolstered by the memory of the discrimination his father had experienced, he was one of the restaurateurs who signed on to Mayor Allen's plan. On June 25, 1963, Herren's became the first Atlanta eatery to voluntarily desegregate.

The first African Americans invited to dine at Herren's were physician Lee Raymond Shelton; his wife, Delores; and her mother, Alberta Walker, who enjoyed a quiet lunch. Lee Shelton recalled the occasion as remarkably ordinary: Negri "sat us in a nice spot in the middle of the restaurant. I ordered beef, it was the best piece of meat I've ever had. It didn't appear that our presence was making any waves or creating any excitement. We ate and looked around the restaurant and the lobster aquarium, then came back home." At the same time, the moment was quite extraordinary: Delores Shelton had been accustomed to going downtown and buying shoes for her four children but not being permitted to use a restroom; the meal at Herren's represented a significant shift in her standing in the city.[1]

The decision to desegregate also had significant consequences for Ye Olde Herren's. It became a target for segregationist protests organized by future Georgia governor Lester Maddox. Picketers walked up and down Luckie Street holding signs that read

DO NOT EAT HERE
THE OWNER OF THIS BUSINESS
IS A LEADER FOR INTEGRATION

In the face of direct threats from Maddox as well as anonymous bomb threats, the Negris sent their children up north for the summer of 1963.

In addition, the restaurant suffered huge losses during 1963—$50,000 (approximately $400,000 today)—and began what became a downward trajectory. With integration gaining steam as a result of the passage of the Civil Rights Act of 1964, Atlanta experienced substantial white flight. Downtown Atlanta emptied out, and so did the business lunch crowd. In 1987, Herren's took its final bow.

Eighteen years and a $5 million renovation later, the curtain rose again on 84 Luckie Street. Peg and Bill Balzer had bought the building in 2002 for $1.2 million and donated it to Atlanta's second-oldest professional theater company, Theatrical Outfit. Through the generosity of the Balzers and other leaders, the building became the two-hundred seat Balzer Theater at Herren's.

Theatrical Outfit had been on a real-estate journey of its own since its 1976 founding in an abandoned laundromat in Atlanta's Virginia Highland neighborhood by artists who had met at the

University of Georgia. The ensemble subsequently helped restore the historic Kress five and dime store near Tenth and Peachtree Streets in Midtown before moving to the Fourteenth Street Playhouse, also in Midtown. In 1995, Tom Key became Theatrical Outfit's artistic director, helping to guide the company down the path that eventually led to Herren's.

Each opening night, Theatrical Outfit serves cinnamon rolls using Herren's original recipe, a sweet homage to the Negri family and to the building's past. The Sheltons became longtime season ticket holders, prompting Lee Shelton to marvel at the rewards of a simple action: "We were very pleased to . . . see that beautiful place, and when we go there now, we really enjoy just sitting in that theater."[2]

# National Center for Civil and Human Rights

## CENTENNIAL OLYMPIC PARK

The eyes of the world turned to Atlanta during the 1996 Summer Olympic Games. Ten thousand participating athletes, 2 million visitors, and 3.5 billion fans tuning in across the globe celebrated and witnessed history being made. At the opening ceremonies, Muhammad Ali lit the cauldron, and Gladys Knight sang "Georgia on My Mind." On the tennis court, Andre Agassi won gold; Michael Johnson burned up the track; Amy Van Dyken earned four gold medals in the pool; and gymnast Kerri Strug stuck a one-foot landing on a vault to cement the first women's gymnastics team gold medal for the United States. Twenty-four countries made their Summer Olympic debuts, including eleven former Soviet republics proudly participating for the first time as independent nations.

For Atlanta, the $1.7 billion investment in hosting the Games paid major dividends, ushering in an era of international prominence and real estate profits. Downtown Atlanta alone realized $2.2 billion in development as a result, including a $75 million catalyst for revitalization in the form of Centennial Olympic Park, which was transformed from a brownfield site into a focal point for locals and visitors and ultimately a home for major attractions, including the National Center for Civil and Human Rights. The center opened in 2014, providing concerts, author talks, educational programming, and intergenerational exhibitions. In addition, the center houses and makes available to the public the papers and artifacts of Dr. Martin Luther King Jr., a short Atlanta Streetcar ride away from the King Birth Home, the King Center, and Sweet Auburn's rich history and culture.

The Atlanta Committee for the Olympic Games faced a herculean challenge when it chose to go up against Athens, Greece, home of the first modern games and spiritual home of the Olympic movement, to host the centennial event. Georgia's Confederate shame and history of segregation presented another major obstacle.

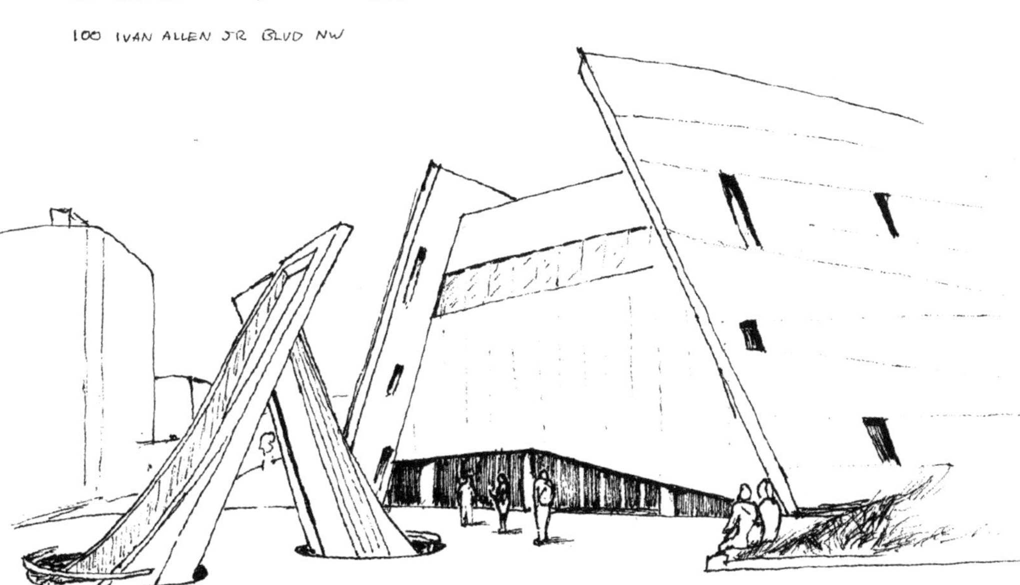

But Mayor Andrew Young, a veteran civil rights activist who worked with King, helped turn this history into an advantage:

> We used to say in the '60s we were a "city too busy to hate." And nobody [in the Olympic movement] believed us because they said, "You're just like everybody else," which was true. Until they came here and they realized we were working together. And were a city that was ethnically diverse, male and female, and we were all in it together as volunteers. And that was unusual: people remarked that we went about this different than anybody had ever done it before.[1]

Eighteen years after the Olympics, Young joined one of his successors in the mayor's office, Shirley Franklin, the first woman to hold the post in Atlanta, to dedicate another monument that combined the legacies of civil rights and Olympic ambition. At

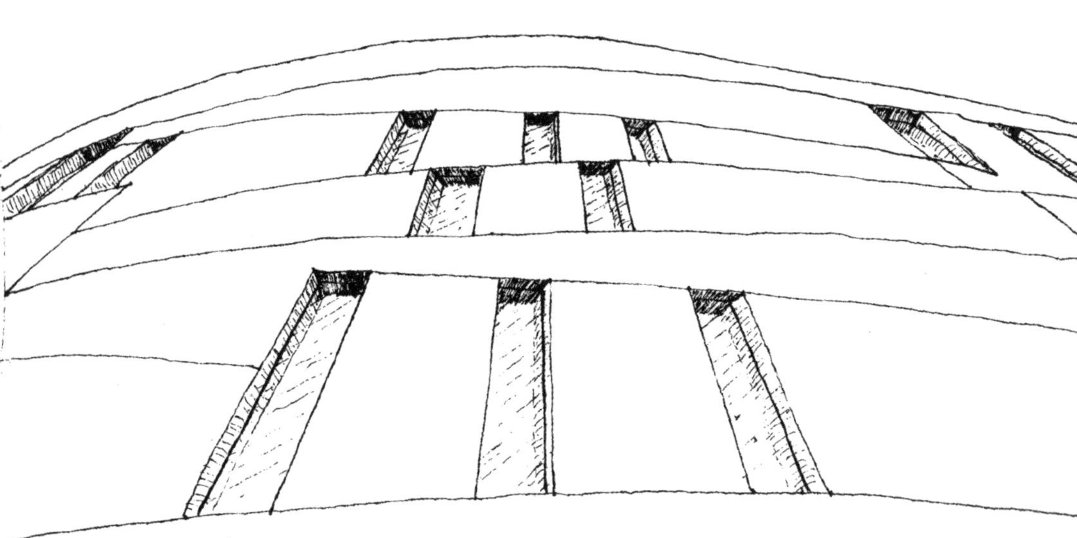

forty-two thousand square feet, the National Center for Civil and Human Rights was built by hometown construction mainstays H. J. Russell & Company, C. D. Moody, and Holder. HOK and the Freelon Group (now part of Perkins & Will) crafted the design, winning a 2008 competition by focusing on the conceptual themes of harmony and solidarity.

In that spirit, the design also references civil and human rights landmarks from around the world, including the National Mall in Washington, D.C.; Tiananmen Square in Beijing; and Tahrir Square in Cairo. These references were an aspirational touch from one of the best-regarded Black architects of his generation, Phil Freelon. Freelon was also the architect of record for the Smithsonian National Museum of African American History and Culture in Washington, D.C., built two years after the center.

Author talks, conversations, and advocacy training are just a few of the ways that the Center illustrates the sacrifice and struggle of the Civil Rights Movement as well as its triumphs and the work yet to be done. The museum offers a deep immersion in domestic and international human rights history, not only instilling knowledge but inspiring activism. Through poignant exhibitions, visitors can learn about *Brown v. Board of Education*, experience a simulated lunch counter sit-in, and examine the immense challenges in the fight for freedom that continues today in the United States and abroad.

The center extends the Civil Rights Movement's ethos of courageous cooperation, heroic action, and dedication to a promise and a dream in the face of daunting challenges with programming for families and advocates of all ages. It has increased its offerings since the nationwide protests over racial equity erupted in 2020, providing direction, structure, and support for people who seek to plan rallies. Interested in getting involved? March on!

## AN OVERVIEW

*Understanding Sweet Auburn also requires understanding the broader Old Fourth Ward neighborhood as well as how people connect to Sweet Auburn in both the past and the present.*

*In this chapter, you'll get a bird's eye view of the landscape, learn about the ups and downs of mass transit in Atlanta, take a tour of one of the country's largest urban infrastructure projects, and conclude with an uplifting and contemplative story about protectors and the protected.*

*These essays provide essential background information in a retroactive manner that helps conclude our story. And since you can read the chapters in Civil Sights and explore Sweet Auburn in any order you like, you might just learn about these spaces and places first!*

CHAPTER 6

# OLD FOURTH WARD

*Atlanta History and a Neighborhood in Flux*

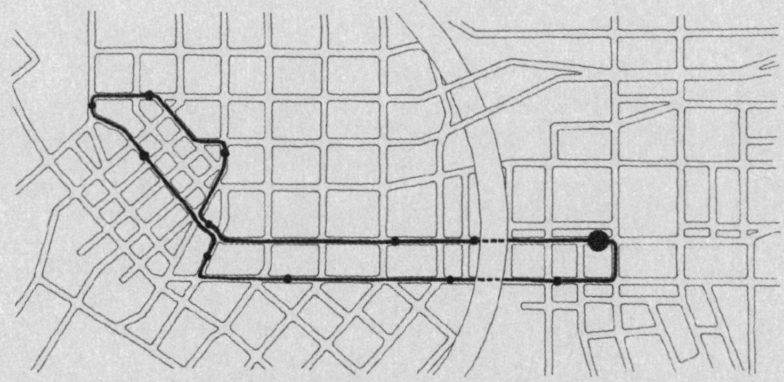

ATLANTA STREETCAR STOP: KING HISTORIC DISTRICT
10-15 MINUTE WALK TO SIGHTS BELOW

**ABOUT O4W**

**KING MEMORIAL MARTA STATION**
377 DECATUR STREET SE

**THE ATLANTA BELTLINE**
ACCESS FROM IRWIN STREET NE

**OLD FOURTH WARD WATER TOWER AND STUDIOPLEX**
659 AUBURN AVENUE

# About O4W

One of Atlanta's oldest sections, the Old Fourth Ward dates back to the Reconstruction years immediately following the Civil War, when the still-young city began to expand rapidly. As early as the 1890s, residents of what was then known simply as the Fourth Ward, especially those in the beautiful homes fronting Boulevard, lived in what some called one of the most desirable areas of the city.

The area affectionately called O4W now encompasses the Martin Luther King Jr. Historical Park and Sweet Auburn and is bordered by Piedmont Avenue to the west, the Atlanta BeltLine to the east, Ponce de Leon Avenue to the north, and the MARTA Blue/Green Line and Oakland Cemetery to the south. Prior to 1954, when the city abandoned the ward system of political districting, the Fourth Ward included an even larger segment of Atlanta's east side. Unlike most of the city's neighborhoods, which were divided into Black, white, and mixed-race sections in accordance with the segregated housing policies of white-run Atlanta, the Fourth Ward started with a mix of Black and white residents living in close proximity.

Sweet Auburn's demographics and culture mirrored the rest of the neighborhood until 1906, when Black residents responded to the Atlanta Massacre by moving into this smaller area in hopes of gaining protection. Black businesses proliferated in Sweet Auburn from the 1910s onward and particularly after the Great Fire of 1917,

LOTTAFRUTTA
590 AUBURN AVE
LOTTA FRUTTA
GOURMET FRUIT HOUSE AND MARKET

which destroyed nearly 1.5 linear miles of property, including some of the handsome old homes on Boulevard.

True to Atlanta's rising-from-the-ashes ambitions, rebuilding occurred. Brick replaced wood, and housing developments became more substantial in both form and function. By 1963, with the Civil Rights Movement in full force, redlining still in effect, and white flight accelerating, almost all of the residents of Sweet Auburn and the Old Fourth Ward were African American.

And then there was the Downtown Connector. In a striking example of infrastructural racism, the new interstate deliberately cut through the heart of Sweet Auburn and other Black neighborhoods, fracturing carefully constructed block patterns along with communities and generations of social ties. Construction had begun in 1948, and the final section opened to traffic in September 1964, at the same time that the passage of the Civil Rights Act was beginning to expand opportunities for Black residents, who moved out of the neighborhood and into other parts of the city and metro area. At the same time that Atlanta as a whole was on the rise, Sweet Auburn was on the decline. Many buildings fell into disrepair.

Atlanta's meteoric growth in the 1980s and 1990s, spurred in part by the 1996 Olympics, helped restore the city center and adjacent neighborhoods and kick-started a reversal of Atlanta's urban exodus. People moved back into the city, seeking neighborhoods with historic character and charm. In the Old Fourth Ward, plans for the Atlanta BeltLine's Eastside Trail promised new experiences, restaurants, and shops, with advocates also pointing to the prospect of improved physical and social mobility. Especially after the Great Recession of 2007–9, outside investment poured into the Old Fourth Ward, resulting in revitalization, though it was unfortunately accompanied by gentrification and displacement.

Today, Sweet Auburn and O4W remain primarily Black, although the percentage of white residents is rising. Black families that have lived there for generations often find themselves priced out of the neighborhood by soaring single-family home values (and the resulting higher property taxes) and rising rents accompanying an upscale building boom.

The neighborhood's progression makes it a fascinating case study on the tensions of balancing investment and inclusion as well as on how historic preservation can be foundational to urban renewal. For example, a former cotton warehouse at 659 Auburn was adapted into Studioplex, which features artists' studios, retail shops, restaurants, and office space. In time, this redevelopment—and the BeltLine—helped catalyze a surging wave of new development to the tune of hundreds of millions of dollars.

A late 1990s adaptive reuse project by the Historic District Development Corporation, which counted Coretta Scott King among its founders, the development helped move vagrants and drug dealers out of the area and provided tantalizing glimpses of a more prosperous future. Now home to boutique shops and restaurants beneath million-dollar townhomes, Studioplex has proven irresistible to the higher-income residents and entrepreneurial businesses, creating a thriving live-work community.

The Old Fourth Ward is a complex and multilayered space, with many issues to contemplate and many places to explore. An understanding of O4W provides history and context for the complicated present in Sweet Auburn and highlights the need for careful navigation of the future.

# King Memorial MARTA Station

## 377 DECATUR STREET SE

Transit has always been a flashpoint for civil rights. A universal need for Black and white city residents alike, public transportation places the two populations in close proximity with one another and thus was a primary venue for segregation. Just two decades removed from the Civil War, journalist Ida B. Wells sued the railroads in Memphis, Tennessee, after she was physically thrown out of the "ladies' car" and off the train, setting off a series of events that inspired Black residents to move West. Building on courageous acts like hers, the modern Civil Rights Movement similarly used transit as a prominent backdrop for civil disobedience, starting with Rosa Parks's 1955 refusal to give up a seat on a bus that sparked the Montgomery Bus Boycott.

Segregation in public transit officially ended in 1959, but true integration did not occur until after the passage of the Civil Rights Act of 1964, title VI of which declared, "No person in the United States shall, on the ground of race, color, or national origin, be excluded from participation in, be denied the benefits of, or be subjected to discrimination under any program or activity receiving Federal financial assistance." In 1965, the same year that civil rights activists marched from Selma to Montgomery in support of voting rights, the Georgia General Assembly voted to form the

Metropolitan Atlanta Rapid Transit Authority (MARTA), which officially began operating in 1966.

MARTA now operates four rail lines with a total of thirty-eight stations. King Memorial was completed in 1979 and is situated on the Blue and Green Lines, which run east to west. The station serves as a node for both train and bus service to Georgia State University, Sweet Auburn, and other parts of downtown. Classified by MARTA as a neighborhood station, King Memorial has an elevated platform that overlooks the forty-eight acres of historic Oakland Cemetery, the city's first public park and the final resting place for seventy thousand people, including Confederate soldiers, enslaved people, Jews, *Gone with the Wind* author Margaret Mitchell, country music star Kenny Rogers, golfing legend Bobby Jones, and poor people in unmarked graves. Among the respected leaders and politicians interred there are Ivan Allen Jr., mayor of Atlanta during the Civil Rights Movement; Sam Massell Jr., the city's first Jewish mayor, who helped lay the foundation for MARTA's expansion while in office; and Maynard Jackson Jr., Atlanta's first Black mayor.

However, the story of mass transit in Atlanta did not begin with MARTA. A century earlier, other modes of municipal transportation traversed Atlanta streets, newly bustling with post–Civil War commerce. Beginning in 1871, commercial horse-drawn wagons elevated members of the upper class away from the manure-strewn streets and quickly and conveniently reach destinations. Mules handled the hot climate better than horses and were deployed on a line running from downtown's Five Points to Whitehorse Tavern, a village in what is now West End. In the 1880s, electric streetcars replaced these mule-drawn trolley cars.

KING MEMORIAL STATION

Many of the early transit companies were linked to real estate developers who had bought rural land and attempted to increase its value by improving accessibility. In 1886, Joel Hurt formed the Atlanta & Edgewood Street Railroad Company, an endeavor that led to the creation of Atlanta's first planned suburb, Inman Park, three years later. According to an 1896 issue of the *Atlanta Constitution*,

> High up above the city, where the purest breezes and the brightest sunshine drove away the germs of disease, and where nature had lavished her best gifts, the gentlemen who conceived the thought of Inman Park found the locality above all others which they desired. It was to be a place of homes, of pretty homes, green lawns, and desirable inhabitants.[1]

Energetic and sometimes speculative businessmen developed many other neighborhoods based on their views of what constituted a richer and cleaner life. Beginning in 1884, a horsecar line connected the Fourth Ward to downtown Atlanta, leading to the construction of new residences along Wheat Street (later Auburn Avenue). At first, Black and white riders commonly sat next to each other, but in 1891, Atlanta passed a law requiring segregation on streetcars "as much as practicable," with enforcement falling to the conductors. Atlanta's streetcar network grew to encompass more than two hundred miles of track by 1949, when the final streetcar line gave way to more mobile trolleys and buses.

In the 1960s, with the emergence of the era of car culture, the city built the Downtown Connector, a massive interstate highway that cut through Atlanta's core. As in many other cities, white planners deliberately routed these new highways through Black neighborhoods: the Downtown Connector bisected Sweet Auburn, disrupting the neighborhood grids, fracturing the community, and imperiling the area's history.

Unlike the highways, public transportation has benefited people from all walks of life, and MARTA has been a major contributor to access in Atlanta. Contemporary transit decisions have focused on more than simply getting people from one point to another, seeking to connect people and neighborhoods, promote businesses, and foster the city's art scene.

As a reflection on history, civil rights, and the promise of Atlanta, MARTA commissioned acclaimed artist Fahamu Pecou to paint four murals at stations in 2016 as part of the En Route program. The first one to be unveiled, *Rise Above,* is located on the Decatur Street side of King Memorial and evokes Martin Luther King Jr.'s words: "An individual has not started living until he can rise above the narrow confines of his individualistic concerns to the broader concerns of all humanity."

Construction of a new streetcar system serving downtown Atlanta and Sweet Auburn began in 2012, with the Atlanta Streetcar opening in December 2014. Now operated by MARTA, the 2.7-mile route has twelve stops between the Martin Luther King Jr. National Historical Park in the east to Centennial Olympic Park in the west. The best thing about the beautifully designed streetcar is that it allows riders to enjoy the places and spaces along the way. Grab a ticket, hop on board, and experience the history!

# The Atlanta BeltLine

For thousands of years, Creek peoples inhabited what is now the Buckhead area of Atlanta, Georgia, with a small village, Standing Peachtree, located where Peachtree Creek meets the Chattahoochee River. The first permanent European settlers began to arrive in the area in the first half of the eighteenth century, bringing with them guns, trade, and disease.

A hundred years later, and with a desire for agricultural and economic expansion, the U.S. government banished the Creeks and other Native peoples from Georgia with passage of the 1830 Indian Removal Act, signed into law by President Andrew Jackson. Over the next two decades, an estimated sixty thousand people were evicted from their ancestral lands in the east and forced to walk to Indian Territory west of the Mississippi River, a journey now known as the Trail of Tears during which thousands died.

Atlanta's history and that of the railroads have always been inextricably intertwined. With the expulsion of Native Americans complete, in 1836, the Georgia General Assembly approved a rail connection from Savannah to the Midwest, with the initial Western & Atlantic Railroad route going from Chattanooga, Tennessee, to a point on the Chattahoochee River near what is now downtown Atlanta's Five Points MARTA station. This small settlement was originally called Terminus and briefly became Marthasville before being renamed Atlanta and officially

EAST SIDE BELTLINE TRAIL

incorporated on December 29, 1847. Nearly two centuries later, reimagining the city's logistical infrastructure may hold the keys to an equitably connected future.

The development of the Atlanta BeltLine, one of the country's most ambitious urban infrastructure projects, officially commenced in 2005. The not-yet-completed twenty-two-mile loop of paved trails follows the path of four former rail lines located on what were then the outskirts of the city. With Atlanta long since having expanded beyond those borders, the BeltLine offers an in-town path for walkers, joggers, commuters, and cyclists around which can be found restaurants, mixed-use developments, public art, skateboard parks, graffiti, public green space, impromptu poetry, lantern parades, grocery stores, beer gardens, skyline views, and all-around urban energy.

The project ultimately will connect forty-five in-town neighborhoods while expanding parks and green space by 40 percent, though development will take longer than the original twenty-year timeline. Ryan Gravel conceived the BeltLine for his 1999 master's thesis at Georgia Tech, and he brought the idea to life with support from Atlanta's neighborhoods and from city council president Cathy Woolard. The BeltLine has already helped generate more than $6.2 billion in new private development. To Gravel and supporters of mass transit along the route, at stake is a fundamental rethinking of what mobility, affordability, and equal opportunity can mean in a city with a storied civil rights and railway history where more recent history has been built around the car.

Transportation infrastructure has become something of a hot topic in Atlanta, but none of these battles has yet been as transformative or violent as the Civil War fight over the city's rail supply lines, which were essential to Confederate logistics. The Union military campaign to take control of those supply lines culminated in the Battle of Atlanta, which began on July 22, 1864. Union general William Tecumseh Sherman laid siege to the city, ultimately forcing Confederate general John Bell Hood to abandon Atlanta on September 1 and then burning it to the ground. The battle was a turning point in the war and in American history. President Abraham Lincoln was up for reelection that fall, and his opponent, former Union general George B. McClellan, a Democrat, ran on a peace platform, contending that the war could not be won and calling for an armistice. The fall of Atlanta proved otherwise, boosting northern morale and helping Lincoln win a second term. Within a few months, the Union army had crushed the southern rebellion.

In a city where roads and bridges have been blamed for deepening divisions rather than serving as human connectors, the BeltLine seeks a different legacy, bringing people together and fostering economic development, cultural diversity, public health, affordable housing, and the environment. It is also a model of smart growth for cities around the world. The BeltLine enables visitors and residents to stroll, roll, run, and ride to such Sweet Auburn and O4W favorites as the Krog Street Market, the Old Fourth Ward Water Tower, Studioplex, Lotta Frutta, and the Martin Luther King Jr. National Historical Park. Hop on and off the trail to witness history, experience culture, and grab a bite, enjoying a bit of fresh air along the way.

OLD FOURTH WARD WATER TOWER

# Old Fourth Ward Water Tower and Studioplex

**659 AUBURN AVENUE**

Visitors approaching Auburn Avenue from the BeltLine first see a tall, concrete water tower on a large patch of grass, an inadvertent beacon of preservation. Across the street, businesses, residences, and creative talent coexist at Studioplex, an urban experiment from the late 1990s that helped revitalize the neighborhood. The Old Fourth Ward Water Tower and the former warehouse it protected represent a story of cotton, race relations, and a nonprofit designed to help preserve the fabric of a community in peril.

In the late 1800s, the east end of Auburn Avenue was an industrial area still in part bound to the cotton industry, a system of white wealth creation relying on Black exploitation. Although activism was already stirring among those who believed that all people are created equal and who were willing to make sacrifices for the Black and poor communities, an organized movement for civil rights must have seemed a long way off.

In 1895, the Atlanta Cotton States and International Exposition was held where Piedmont Park sits today. The exposition's foundational idea was to showcase southern post–Civil War economic progress as a means of bolstering domestic business and international trade. At the opening ceremonies, Booker T. Washington, who had been born into slavery and who had overcome astonishing odds to become one of the most celebrated leaders

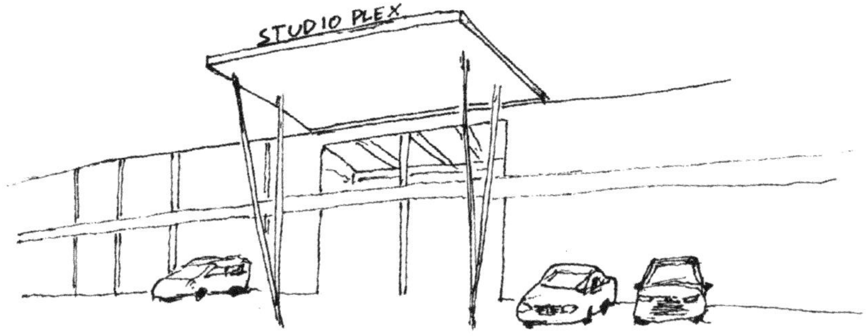


in American history, delivered perhaps his most famous speech, drawing both criticism and commendation. White promoters had invited Washington to show progress in race relations and to entice the predominantly white audience to invest in a new future.

At the time, Black people represented one-third of the South's population, and Washington argued that their inclusion in the region's industrialization would benefit everyone. He clearly viewed this as a pragmatic approach that took into account the biases of the day, which he knew would preclude full integration. "In all things that are purely social we can be as separate as the fingers, yet one as the hand in all things essential to mutual progress," Washington famously proclaimed. Some Black activists found his speech too conciliatory and labeled the speech "The Atlanta Compromise," but for the mostly white audience, Washington's words pointed to a pathway that promised racial cooperation without full equality or instability.

Subsequent events validated the concerns of Washington's Black critics. The U.S. Supreme Court's 1896 *Plessy v. Ferguson* decision legitimized the "separate but equal" doctrine that reinforced segregation. Then came the 1906 Atlanta Massacre, in which white mobs rampaged through the streets, killing Black people just a few miles from where Washington had appealed for peaceful coexistence.

Meanwhile, however, the cotton industry continued to prosper, and the Atlantic Compress Company's factory at 659 Auburn Avenue needed a fire-suppression system. In 1906, Piedmont Construction built a one-hundred-foot-tall water tower at the corner of Sampson and Irwin Streets. Engineered by H. H. Johnson, the 100,000-gallon suppression system used gravity to fill sprinklers. In June 1909, three years after it was built, the water tower proved its usefulness when the factory went up in flames, dousing the fire, and making possible the site's continued use, and preserving its future potential. Through Prohibition, the Great Depression, two world wars, and the Civil Rights Movement, what is now thought to be Atlanta's oldest surviving water tower remained intact even as the surrounding neighborhood decayed. By the 1970s, the defunct warehouse had become a magnet for vagrants and drug dealers.

Sweet Auburn became a National Historic Landmark in 1976, and four years later, Coretta Scott King and Christine King Farris founded the Historic District Development Corporation to protect homes and buildings in the neighborhood. The corporation initially focused on residences around the Martin Luther King Jr. Birth Home Block, but its founders had a broader vision. Mtamanika Youngblood, the organization's first executive director, pitched a plan for the adaptive reuse of the old cotton warehouse, and Studioplex was born. Completed in 2000, the $18.3 million project brought together Blacks and whites, artists and real estate agents, hairstylists and gallery owners in 225,000 square feet of live-work

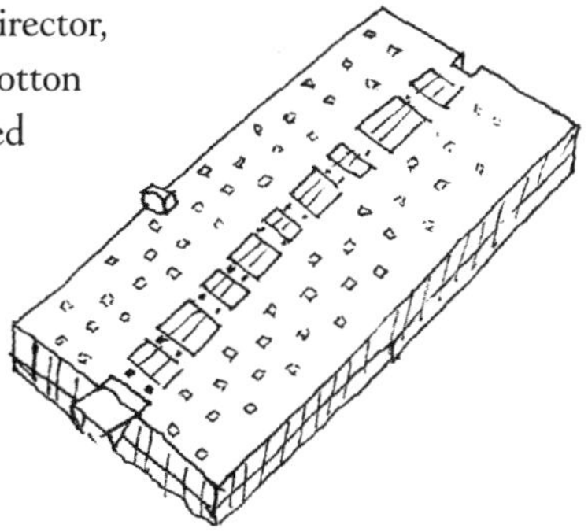

STUDIOPLEX

loft space and open air. Today, Studioplex has 112 residential lofts, 41 commercial spaces, and ample vitality.

Via Studioplex's success and a renewed focus on preservation, the water tower went from protector to protected, and the neighborhood began to draw businesses and visitors by the hundreds of thousands.

Looking for somewhere to go next? Cross the Atlanta BeltLine's Eastside Trail and walk a block to the Food Hall at the Krog Street Market. Try a pastry from the Little Tart Bakeshop, a burger from Fred's Meat & Bread, a slice from Varuni Napoli, or a cone from Jeni's Ice Cream, then come back and picnic in the Old Water Tower Park, basking in Sweet Auburn's storied history.

# Afterword

**JACQUELINE JONES ROYSTER**
*Professor Emerita at the Ohio State University and Georgia Institute of Technology*

*Civil Sights* is a remarkable collection of short essays that highlight places and spaces that are part of Atlanta's Sweet Auburn district in the Old Fourth Ward. The sites highlighted here confirm the incredible vibrancy of this historic African American community as well as the striking number of places in this area that have been quite deeply integrative in the lives of generations of people who have lived and worked there and who have utilized and enjoyed various resources along these streets, including me. I did not live in Atlanta as a youth. My home was a small town farther east in the state. Even so, for a whole range of reasons, I spent a substantial amount of time in Old Fourth Ward in the homes of close relatives—aunts, uncles, and cousins who had come to call the area home and who had come to see Sweet Auburn as setting the tone for the quality of their lives.

As a child coming of age in the 1960s in a close-knit family during a time of social and political change, I was privileged to be within this cultural space quite regularly—on weekends, for several weeks each summer, on holidays, and more. Over time, I have come to understand that I was being imprinted with experiences and memories that live with me still. *Civil Sights* captures the spirit of these memories and sets them within a context that affirms the richness of history and culture I witnessed, even as a visitor.

The list of places in the Sweet Auburn District that mattered to me personally as I was growing up is really quite long, and I am very pleased to see that my special sites are well reflected in *Civil Sights*. They include the iconic Big Bethel African Methodist Episcopal Church, the flagship in the state of Georgia for my family's faith traditions. Big Bethel represented the power of spiritual belief as well as a profound sense of resilience, beauty of place and purpose, and pride. Even as a child, this place was for me a symbol of belonging; it made it clear that the important people who occupied this building were my people and that I would be recognized and welcomed among them.

My special places also include the Curb Market, filled with its collection of meats and vegetables and well-presented treats of various kinds. It was a personal favorite for my father, and I treasure the times that I spent with him and my mother there. I was their tagalong partner in consumerism, and they passed down to me a deep appreciation for conveniently available farm-to-buyer options. We delighted in having such good access to a dependable resource for fresh and healthy foods. My special places also included my aunt's beauty salon, where my mother occasionally had my hair done. In the salon, I felt luxuriously treated by my aunt's hairstylist friend, but what I remember most was that the salon was on the second floor and that the building had the most remarkable marble staircase that I had ever seen.

There were many other meaning-filled sites as well. As my cousins and I were growing up, one place was the Yates & Milton Drugstore, where we were permitted to buy Cherry Cokes and occasionally snacks. At the time, I had no clue of its distinctiveness in the history of health care resources for African Americans in Atlanta or in the state. Another place was Hughes Spalding Hospital, near the Curb Market, the designated public hospital for the care of African American citizens. When I was six years old, my African American physician's office was in Atlanta, not in my hometown, and he removed my tonsils at Hughes Spalding. Yet another site was the Bell Street Girls Club. A summer program there arranged for my first swimming lesson at the Butler Street YMCA, and to this day I still have a problem remembering that this building was the YMCA, not the YWCA.

My aunt was an agent for the Atlanta Life Insurance Company. Occasionally, my cousins and I would ride along with her as she engaged with her clients, and we understood even as young children that the insurance business was important for our family. Important also was that my family members were loyal subscribers to the *Atlanta Daily World*, which became a linchpin in keeping my parents (and eventually me) informed about issues, challenges, and opportunities. "Our" Atlanta newspaper (along with the *Pittsburgh Courier*, *Ebony* magazine, and *Jet* magazine) was a key tool for our knowing about the world from a community-centered view beyond my small town and for knowing that there were always events and accomplishments related to the African American experience to actually celebrate. In reflection, I now understand in quite an affirming way that my family was part of the broadly defined story—the impressive reading audience—that the *Atlanta Daily World* generated as a pioneering periodical with both local and national history and impact.

Moreover, my father was a Prince Hall Mason and my mother was an Eastern Star. While these "secret" organizations were quite a mystery to me, I was aware enough to take note that Auburn Avenue had an impressive Prince Hall Masons building that my young mind associated with a brotherhood that my father treasured and that was part of my dad's extended circle of friends. In similar fashion, I lived

vicariously through my closest Old Fourth Ward cousin. She was a Girl Scout. My small town had no African American Girl Scout troop, so that association was not available to me, but I was proud to see her all dressed up in her uniforms from her Brownie days through the many activities that led her to full Girl Scout status. I found her life as a city girl interesting and adventurous and worthy of my admiration. Her Girl Scout troop met on Auburn Avenue.

When we look back with a critical eye at the vibrancy on so many levels of Sweet Auburn as both real and idealized space, the impact of its vitality is quite stunning. In addition to being in simple terms a generator of my childhood memories, this district was also a place that facilitated a broadening of my cultural awareness. I was a country child who knew only Methodists, Baptists, Presbyterians, and just two Jewish families: of the first Catholics that I met was at the Bell Street Girls Club. She went to school and church at Our Lady of Lourdes. I found that fact fascinating—so much so, in fact, that I still think about her each time that I pass by Our Lady of Lourdes. I also took notice of the Royal Peacock. I know it now as a pioneering and pacesetting site for music and entertainment. At the time, however, its striking black-and-red design and its bold peacock image were emblazoned in my imagination. For me, it was a curious place. It became real not as a nightclub but as a place managed by the father of two girls who lived down the street from my cousins and with whom they played. What stood out was that on a couple of occasions when we were playing in their home, African American performers passed through. Even I knew who B. B. King was, and I was impressed that I could be in a neighborhood where he was performing but where his presence just felt normal.

In many ways, experiences such as these made Sweet Auburn feel more like home than my actual hometown did. Atlanta and its community have loomed large in my experiences, my memories, and my imagination. In effect, Sweet Auburn was a place not only for generations of residents but also for generations of visitors. Sweet Auburn was a community that I could authentically claim, and it was a testament to the strength, ingenuity, resourcefulness, talents, joy, love, pride, and tenacity of its residents and visitors. As an African American child, I was deeply affirmed by this richly endowed ecosystem.

As an adult and a professional in the academic arena, however, I recognize that Sweet Auburn was confronted regularly by serious challenges to its survival as a vibrant community. I have endured periods of deep sadness as I have witnessed—for example, during my college days at the Atlanta University Center and later during my first days as a professor—that some of the specific places and spaces that were so much a part of my sense of history and community well-being were experiencing dramatic downturns, downturns that we typically describe as disinvestment and abandonment and as gentrification. With *Civil Sights*, however, I am reminded that as a built environment, Sweet Auburn has succeeded in holding its place as the proverbial heartbeat of one of Atlanta's oldest and largest African American communities, a fact that brings me both comfort and hope. I have the comfort of knowing how strong and resilient people of African descent have been in Atlanta, and I harbor the hope and expectation of ongoing success that is nourished by a continuous commitment to community action and sustainability. Not only has Sweet Auburn retained critical community resources (such as Big Bethel and other churches, the Prince Hall Masons, and the Curb Market), but key preservation projects have emerged (for example, the expansive Martin Luther King Jr. National Historical Park). In addition, many spaces are being repurposed (for example, the *Atlanta Daily World* Building, the Southern School Book Building) in support of new and different business enterprises. In fact, in recent decades, newer projects have come alive and rooted themselves within the life of the community—restaurants and living spaces; the APEX Museum; Georgia State University; and the newly renovated Auburn Avenue Research Library on African American Culture and History, a community resource that is distinctive not only as a local asset, but as a national and international institution. The contemporary landscape of Sweet Auburn sites have combined—just as those of the past did—to create sturdy anchors for excellence and for the demonstration of ample signs of life for the future.

*Civil Sights* offers an easily accessible opportunity to gain knowledge about a distinctive community, a place that is carrying forward historical richness and remarkable traditions in business and entrepreneurship, education, arts, music, religion, technology, and more. This volume graciously invites readers to see—to look and listen to—this community for themselves, to learn, and to partake of the resources that remain vital and vibrant. These short essays celebrate the past and the present. They acknowledge the problems and issues that have confronted this community and its sites. They showcase the resilience of a community that continues to stand tall not just for now but for the future. With this story framework, *Civil Sights* reminds us that Sweet Auburn has held its own through thick and thin, with and without consistent or ample civic support. It has endured and it continues to thrive.

I share all of this to say that when Gene Kansas (one of the developers who is helping to renew and revitalize Sweet Auburn and who is helping to create this space's ongoing ascendancy) told me about his desire to publish a book that presents some of the stories of the Sweet Auburn District, I saw it as an absolutely wonderful idea. I believed that all sorts of folks should really know this place and develop a sense of the people who made it and passed it on for future generations. I believe that *Civil Sights* both helps those, like me, who know Sweet Auburn feel affirmed by these accounts of ongoing wonders and encourages those unfamiliar with the area to taste this amazingly diverse urban scene and invites them to learn more. *Civil Sights* honors the past, celebrates the present, and looks toward the future. In so doing, it reminds all of us that places and spaces are part and parcel of who we are and who we might become.

In twenty-first-century Atlanta, we live our lives day to day, month to month, year to year in places and spaces that are leaving imprints on us and our city, just as we are leaving behind our imprints on our famously ever-evolving built environment. It is as if, in living, working, and existing in the spaces around us, we are writing ourselves into the air that we breathe rather than merely onto a wall or a floor. Yes, *we were here*, and, yes, *here* has been and remains truly interesting and inspiring. My sense of nostalgia at participating in the *Civil Sights* project has therefore been incredibly deep, and I am very pleased to see a book that so graciously invites all of us to see and appreciate, to enjoy and be inspired by, an area that embodies who we have been as a city as well as the history of the multiple ways in which a long-standing community has breathed life into a specific set of places and spaces. The short essays reference Sweet Auburn's trials and its tribulations, its sweetness and its light. They declare, as people like me also declare, that there really is just no place quite like Sweet Auburn. I thank Gene for having and following through with such a good and useful idea.

# Curriculum Ideas

## High School and College

1. Perform a close reading of the Oliver Goldsmith poem "The Deserted Village" together as a class (see the appendix). Then instruct students to take a walking tour of Sweet Auburn using this book as a guide, selecting five sites to visit. Write up a report about how the physical environment both matches and diverges from the Goldsmith poem, hypothesizing reasons for both the linkages and divergences.
2. For classes that are making use of GIS or other mapping software, have the students design an interactive map of Sweet Auburn using this text as a guide.
3. To teach citational practices, have the students study the endnotes and additional reading for one or two specific chapters. Students can read sources, create an annotated bibliography, and compare and contrast it to the chapter. What similarities popped up? What differences? What might be the causes and effects of how we choose to cite sources and highlight disparate elements of a particular source?
4. Ask students to create a digital timeline of the growth, decline, and rebirth of Sweet Auburn using this text as a guide. This particular assignment could also be fashioned as a public scholarship project and would work well as a group project.
5. Assign chapters from Jane Jacobs's *The Death and Life of Great American Cities* (one chapter or more per student, depending on the number of students). Have students read their assigned chapter(s) and make connections to *Civil Sights*. Then have students prepare a collaborative report on their assigned sections of the Jacobs text and this guide, bearing in mind historical preservation practices, the built environment, and urban issues.

## Middle School

1. Ask students to select a particular individual from *Civil Sights* and to research the other people in that person's life: for example, Martin Luther King Jr.'s mother and siblings rather than King himself. Students can focus on the importance of community support for the "great men" of history.
2. Take students on a walking tour of the neighborhood, asking each student in advance to act as the guide for a particular stop. Have each students prepare a short presentation for their classmates based on the information in *Civil Sights*.
3. Ask students to draw their conception of a particular site from *Civil Sights*. Then have them view a photo of the site or visit in person. Students can discuss creativity, artistic practices, and urban change through the lens of their own art.

## Elementary School

1. Ask students to select one entry from *Civil Sights* to read on their own or with a parent and then come to class with two or three questions to discuss with their classmates.
2. Develop a field trip around Sweet Auburn, focusing on demonstrating to students that history is embedded into the built environment. Ask students to consider and then discuss what history might be living in their own neighborhoods.

# Appendix

**OLIVER GOLDSMITH, "THE DESERTED VILLAGE," 1770**

*(https://www.poetryfoundation.org/poems/44292/the-deserted-village)*

Sweet Auburn, loveliest village of the plain,
Where health and plenty cheared the labouring swain,
Where smiling spring its earliest visit paid,
And parting summer's lingering blooms delayed,
Dear lovely bowers of innocence and ease,
Seats of my youth, when every sport could please,
How often have I loitered o'er thy green,
Where humble happiness endeared each scene!
How often have I paused on every charm,
The sheltered cot, the cultivated farm,
The never-failing brook, the busy mill,
The decent church that topt the neighbouring hill,
The hawthorn bush, with seats beneath the shade,
For talking age and whispering lovers made!
How often have I blest the coming day,
When toil remitting lent its turn to play,
And all the village train, from labour free,
Led up their sports beneath the spreading tree,
While many a pastime circled in the shade,
The young contending as the old surveyed;
And many a gambol frolicked o'er the ground,
And slights of art and feats of strength went round;

And still as each repeated pleasure tired,
Succeeding sports the mirthful band inspired;
The dancing pair that simply sought renown
By holding out to tire each other down;
The swain mistrustless of his smutted face,
While secret laughter tittered round the place;
The bashful virgin's side-long looks of love,
The matron's glance that would those looks reprove!
These were thy charms, sweet village; sports like these,
With sweet succession, taught even toil to please;
These round thy bowers their chearful influence shed,
These were thy charms—But all these charms are fled.
Sweet smiling village, loveliest of the lawn,
Thy sports are fled, and all thy charms withdrawn;
Amidst thy bowers the tyrant's hand is seen,
And desolation saddens all thy green:
One only master grasps the whole domain,
And half a tillage stints thy smiling plain;
No more thy glassy brook reflects the day,
But, choaked with sedges, works its weedy way;
Along thy glades, a solitary guest,
The hollow-sounding bittern guards its nest;
Amidst thy desert walks the lapwing flies,
And tires their echoes with unvaried cries.
Sunk are thy bowers, in shapeless ruin all,
And the long grass o'ertops the mouldering wall;
And, trembling, shrinking from the spoiler's hand,
Far, far away, thy children leave the land.
Ill fares the land, to hastening ills a prey,
Where wealth accumulates, and men decay:
Princes and lords may flourish, or may fade;
A breath can make them, as a breath has made;
But a bold peasantry, their country's pride,
When once destroyed, can never be supplied.
A time there was, ere England's griefs began,
When every rood of ground maintained its man;
For him light labour spread her wholesome store,
Just gave what life required, but gave no more:
His best companions, innocence and health;
And his best riches, ignorance of wealth.
But times are altered; trade's unfeeling train

Usurp the land and dispossess the swain;
Along the lawn, where scattered hamlets rose,
Unwieldy wealth and cumbrous pomp repose;
And every want to oppulence allied,
And every pang that folly pays to pride.
Those gentle hours that plenty bade to bloom,
Those calm desires that asked but little room,
Those healthful sports that graced the peaceful scene,
Lived in each look, and brightened all the green;
These, far departing seek a kinder shore,
And rural mirth and manners are no more.
Sweet Auburn! parent of the blissful hour,
Thy glades forlorn confess the tyrant's power.
Here as I take my solitary rounds,
Amidst thy tangling walks, and ruined grounds,
And, many a year elapsed, return to view
Where once the cottage stood, the hawthorn grew,
Remembrance wakes with all her busy train,
Swells at my breast, and turns the past to pain.
In all my wanderings round this world of care,
In all my griefs—and God has given my share—
I still had hopes, my latest hours to crown,
Amidst these humble bowers to lay me down;
To husband out life's taper at the close,
And keep the flame from wasting by repose.
I still had hopes, for pride attends us still,
Amidst the swains to shew my book-learned skill,
Around my fire an evening groupe to draw,
And tell of all I felt, and all I saw;
And, as an hare whom hounds and horns pursue,
Pants to the place from whence at first she flew,
I still had hopes, my long vexations past,
Here to return—and die at home at last.
O blest retirement, friend to life's decline,
Retreats from care that never must be mine,
How happy he who crowns, in shades like these
A youth of labour with an age of ease;
Who quits a world where strong temptations try,
And, since 'tis hard to combat, learns to fly!
For him no wretches, born to work and weep,
Explore the mine, or tempt the dangerous deep;

No surly porter stands in guilty state
To spurn imploring famine from the gate,
But on he moves to meet his latter end,
Angels around befriending virtue's friend;
Bends to the grave with unperceived decay,
While resignation gently slopes the way;
And, all his prospects brightening to the last,
His Heaven commences ere the world be past!
Sweet was the sound, when oft at evening's close,
Up yonder hill the village murmur rose;
There, as I past with careless steps and slow,
The mingling notes came soften'd from below;
The swain responsive as the milk-maid sung,
The sober herd that lowed to meet their young,
The noisy geese that gabbled o'er the pool,
The playful children just let loose from school,
The watch-dog's voice that bayed the whispering wind,
And the loud laugh that spoke the vacant mind,
These all in sweet confusion sought the shade,
And filled each pause the nightingale had made.
But now the sounds of population fail,
No cheerful murmurs fluctuate in the gale,
No busy steps the grass-grown foot-way tread,
For all the bloomy flush of life is fled.
All but yon widowed, solitary thing
That feebly bends beside the plashy spring;
She, wretched matron, forced in age, for bread,
To strip the brook with mantling cresses spread,
To pick her wintry faggot from the thorn,
To seek her nightly shed, and weep till morn;
She only left of all the harmless train,
The sad historian of the pensive plain.
Near yonder copse, where once the garden smiled,
And still where many a garden-flower grows wild;
There, where a few torn shrubs the place disclose,
The village preacher's modest mansion rose.
A man he was, to all the country dear,
And passing rich with forty pounds a year;
Remote from towns he ran his godly race,
Nor e'er had changed, nor wished to change his place;
Unpractised he to fawn, or seek for power,

By doctrines fashioned to the varying hour;
Far other aims his heart had learned to prize,
More skilled to raise the wretched than to rise.
His house was known to all the vagrant train,
He chid their wanderings but relieved their pain;
The long-remembered beggar was his guest,
Whose beard descending swept his aged breast;
The ruined spendthrift, now no longer proud,
Claim'd kindred there, and had his claims allowed;
The broken soldier, kindly bade to stay,
Sate by his fire, and talked the night away;
Wept o'er his wounds, or, tales of sorrow done,
Shouldered his crutch, and shewed how fields were won.
Pleased with his guests, the good man learned to glow,
And quite forgot their vices in their woe;
Careless their merits, or their faults to scan,
His pity gave ere charity began.
Thus to relieve the wretched was his pride,
And even his failings leaned to Virtue's side;
But in his duty prompt at every call,
He watched and wept, he prayed and felt, for all.
And, as a bird each fond endearment tries,
To tempt its new-fledged offspring to the skies;
He tried each art, reproved each dull delay,
Allured to brighter worlds, and led the way.
Beside the bed where parting life was layed,
And sorrow, guilt, and pain, by turns, dismayed
The reverend champion stood. At his control
Despair and anguish fled the struggling soul;
Comfort came down the trembling wretch to raise,
And his last faltering accents whispered praise.
At church, with meek and unaffected grace,
His looks adorned the venerable place;
Truth from his lips prevailed with double sway,
And fools, who came to scoff, remained to pray.
The service past, around the pious man,
With steady zeal, each honest rustic ran;
Even children followed, with endearing wile,
And plucked his gown, to share the good man's smile.
His ready smile a parent's warmth exprest,
Their welfare pleased him, and their cares distrest:

To them his heart, his love, his griefs were given,
But all his serious thoughts had rest in Heaven.
As some tall cliff that lifts its awful form,
Swells from the vale, and midway leaves the storm,
Tho' round its breast the rolling clouds are spread,
Eternal sunshine settles on its head.
Beside yon straggling fence that skirts the way,
With blossomed furze unprofitably gay,
There, in his noisy mansion, skill'd to rule,
The village master taught his little school;
A man severe he was, and stern to view,
I knew him well, and every truant knew;
Well had the boding tremblers learned to trace
The day's disasters in his morning face;
Full well they laughed, with counterfeited glee,
At all his jokes, for many a joke had he:
Full well the busy whisper circling round,
Conveyed the dismal tidings when he frowned;
Yet he was kind, or if severe in aught,
The love he bore to learning was in fault;
The village all declared how much he knew;
'Twas certain he could write, and cypher too;
Lands he could measure, terms and tides presage,
And ev'n the story ran that he could gauge.
In arguing too, the parson owned his skill,
For even tho' vanquished, he could argue still;
While words of learned length and thundering sound,
Amazed the gazing rustics ranged around;
And still they gazed, and still the wonder grew,
That one small head could carry all he knew.
But past is all his fame. The very spot
Where many a time he triumphed, is forgot.
Near yonder thorn, that lifts its head on high,
Where once the sign-post caught the passing eye,
Low lies that house where nut-brown draughts inspired,
Where grey-beard mirth and smiling toil retired,
Where village statesmen talked with looks profound,
And news much older than their ale went round.
Imagination fondly stoops to trace
The parlour splendours of that festive place;
The white-washed wall, the nicely sanded floor,

The varnished clock that clicked behind the door;
The chest contrived a double debt to pay,
A bed by night, a chest of drawers by day;
The pictures placed for ornament and use,
The twelve good rules, the royal game of goose;
The hearth, except when winter chill'd the day,
With aspen boughs, and flowers, and fennel gay;
While broken tea-cups, wisely kept for shew,
Ranged o'er the chimney, glistened in a row.
Vain transitory splendours! Could not all
Reprieve the tottering mansion from its fall!
Obscure it sinks, nor shall it more impart
An hour's importance to the poor man's heart;
Thither no more the peasant shall repair
To sweet oblivion of his daily care;
No more the farmer's news, the barber's tale,
No more the woodman's ballad shall prevail;
No more the smith his dusky brow shall clear,
Relax his ponderous strength, and lean to hear;
The host himself no longer shall be found
Careful to see the mantling bliss go round;
Nor the coy maid, half willing to be prest,
Shall kiss the cup to pass it to the rest.
Yes! let the rich deride, the proud disdain,
These simple blessings of the lowly train;
To me more dear, congenial to my heart,
One native charm, than all the gloss of art;
Spontaneous joys, where Nature has its play,
The soul adopts, and owns their first-born sway;
Lightly they frolic o'er the vacant mind,
Unenvied, unmolested, unconfined.
But the long pomp, the midnight masquerade,
With all the freaks of wanton wealth arrayed,
In these, ere triflers half their wish obtain,
The toiling pleasure sickens into pain;
And, even while fashion's brightest arts decoy,
The heart distrusting asks, if this be joy.
Ye friends to truth, ye statesmen who survey
The rich man's joys encrease, the poor's decay,
'Tis yours to judge, how wide the limits stand
Between a splendid and a happy land.

Proud swells the tide with loads of freighted ore,
And shouting Folly hails them from her shore;
Hoards even beyond the miser's wish abound,
And rich men flock from all the world around.
Yet count our gains. This wealth is but a name
That leaves our useful products still the same.
Not so the loss. The man of wealth and pride
Takes up a space that many poor supplied;
Space for his lake, his park's extended bounds,
Space for his horses, equipage, and hounds:
The robe that wraps his limbs in silken sloth,
Has robbed the neighbouring fields of half their growth;
His seat, where solitary sports are seen,
Indignant spurns the cottage from the green:
Around the world each needful product flies,
For all the luxuries the world supplies.
While thus the land adorned for pleasure, all
In barren splendour feebly waits the fall.
As some fair female unadorned and plain,
Secure to please while youth confirms her reign,
Slights every borrowed charm that dress supplies,
Nor shares with art the triumph of her eyes.
But when those charms are past, for charms are frail,
When time advances, and when lovers fail,
She then shines forth, solicitous to bless,
In all the glaring impotence of dress.
Thus fares the land, by luxury betrayed:
In nature's simplest charms at first arrayed;
But verging to decline, its splendours rise,
Its vistas strike, its palaces surprize;
While, scourged by famine from the smiling land,
The mournful peasant leads his humble band;
And while he sinks, without one arm to save,
The country blooms—a garden, and a grave.
Where then, ah where, shall poverty reside,
To scape the pressure of contiguous pride?
If to some common's fenceless limits strayed,
He drives his flock to pick the scanty blade,
Those fenceless fields the sons of wealth divide,
And ev'n the bare-worn common is denied.

If to the city sped—What waits him there?
To see profusion that he must not share;
To see ten thousand baneful arts combined
To pamper luxury, and thin mankind;
To see those joys the sons of pleasure know,
Extorted from his fellow-creature's woe.
Here while the courtier glitters in brocade,
There the pale artist plies the sickly trade;
Here while the proud their long-drawn pomps display,
There the black gibbet glooms beside the way.
The dome where Pleasure holds her midnight reign,
Here, richly deckt, admits the gorgeous train;
Tumultuous grandeur crowds the blazing square,
The rattling chariots clash, the torches glare.
Sure scenes like these no troubles e'er annoy!
Sure these denote one universal joy!
Are these thy serious thoughts?—Ah, turn thine eyes
Where the poor houseless shivering female lies.
She once, perhaps, in village plenty blest,
Has wept at tales of innocence distrest;
Her modest looks the cottage might adorn
Sweet as the primrose peeps beneath the thorn:
Now lost to all; her friends, her virtue fled,
Near her betrayer's door she lays her head,
And, pinch'd with cold, and shrinking from the shower,
With heavy heart deplores that luckless hour
When idly first, ambitious of the town,
She left her wheel and robes of country brown.
Do thine, sweet Auburn, thine, the loveliest train,
Do thy fair tribes participate her pain?
Even now, perhaps, by cold and hunger led,
At proud men's doors they ask a little bread!
Ah, no. To distant climes, a dreary scene,
Where half the convex world intrudes between,
Through torrid tracts with fainting steps they go,
Where wild Altama murmurs to their woe.
Far different there from all that charm'd before,
The various terrors of that horrid shore;
Those blazing suns that dart a downward ray,
And fiercely shed intolerable day;

Those matted woods where birds forget to sing,
But silent bats in drowsy clusters cling;
Those poisonous fields with rank luxuriance crowned,
Where the dark scorpion gathers death around;
Where at each step the stranger fears to wake
The rattling terrors of the vengeful snake;
Where crouching tigers wait their hapless prey,
And savage men, more murderous still than they;
While oft in whirls the mad tornado flies,
Mingling the ravaged landscape with the skies.
Far different these from every former scene,
The cooling brook, the grassy vested green,
The breezy covert of the warbling grove,
That only shelter'd thefts of harmless love.
Good Heaven! what sorrows gloom'd that parting day,
That called them from their native walks away;
When the poor exiles, every pleasure past,
Hung round their bowers, and fondly looked their last,
And took a long farewell, and wished in vain
For seats like these beyond the western main;
And shuddering still to face the distant deep,
Returned and wept, and still returned to weep.
The good old sire the first prepared to go
To new found worlds, and wept for others woe.
But for himself, in conscious virtue brave,
He only wished for worlds beyond the grave.
His lovely daughter, lovelier in her tears,
The fond companion of his helpless years,
Silent went next, neglectful of her charms,
And left a lover's for a father's arms.
With louder plaints the mother spoke her woes,
And blessed the cot where every pleasure rose;
And kist her thoughtless babes with many a tear,
And claspt them close, in sorrow doubly dear;
Whilst her fond husband strove to lend relief
In all the silent manliness of grief.
O luxury! thou curst by Heaven's decree,
How ill exchanged are things like these for thee!
How do thy potions, with insidious joy,
Diffuse their pleasures only to destroy!
Kingdoms, by thee, to sickly greatness grown,

Boast of a florid vigour not their own;
At every draught more large and large they grow,
A bloated mass of rank unwieldy woe;
Till sapped their strength, and every part unsound,
Down, down they sink, and spread a ruin round.
Even now the devastation is begun,
And half the business of destruction done;
Even now, methinks, as pondering here I stand,
I see the rural virtues leave the land:
Down where yon anchoring vessel spreads the sail,
That idly waiting flaps with every gale,
Downward they move, a melancholy band,
Pass from the shore, and darken all the strand.
Contented toil, and hospitable care,
And kind connubial tenderness, are there;
And piety with wishes placed above,
And steady loyalty, and faithful love.
And thou, sweet Poetry, thou loveliest maid,
Still first to fly where sensual joys invade;
Unfit in these degenerate times of shame,
To catch the heart, or strike for honest fame;
Dear charming nymph, neglected and decried,
My shame in crowds, my solitary pride;
Thou source of all my bliss, and all my woe,
That found'st me poor at first, and keep'st me so;
Thou guide by which the nobler arts excell,
Thou nurse of every virtue, fare thee well!
Farewell, and O where'er thy voice be tried,
On Torno's cliffs, or Pambamarca's side,
Whether were equinoctial fervours glow,
Or winter wraps the polar world in snow,
Still let thy voice, prevailing over time,
Redress the rigours of the inclement clime;
Aid slighted truth with thy persuasive strain,
Teach erring man to spurn the rage of gain;
Teach him, that states of native strength possest,
Tho' very poor, may still be very blest;
That trade's proud empire hastes to swift decay,
As ocean sweeps the labour'd mole away;
While self-dependent power can time defy,
As rocks resist the billows and the sky.

# THE FIRST EIGHT BLACK POLICE OFFICERS IN ATLANTA, APRIL 1948

WILLIE T ELKINS

WILLARD STRICKLAND

ROBERT MCKIBBENS

JOHNNIE P JONES

CLAUDE DIXON

JOHN SANDERS

HENRY HOOKS

ERNEST H LYONS

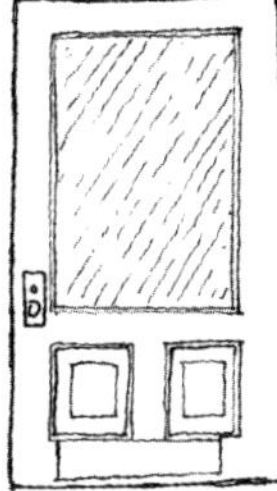

# Notes

## Chapter 1. The Birth Home Block

### CHARLES LINCOLN HARPER HOUSE

1. "Charles Lincoln Harper (1877–1955), Inspiring Principal and Activist: 'A Man with a Vision,'" Harper-Archer Elementary School, accessed December 28, 2023, https://www.atlantapublicschools.us/Page/60053.

2. "Charles Lincoln Harper."

### HAMILTON HOWELL HOUSE

1. Arthur Bunyan Caldwell, "Alexander Daniel Hamilton," in *History of the American Negro and His Institutions, Georgia Edition* (Atlanta: A. B. Caldwell, 1917), 88, https://babel.hathitrust.org/cgi/pt?id=hvd.32044015579857&view=1up&seq=106&q1=Alexander%20hamilton.

### BRYANT-GRAVES HOUSE

1. *The Voice of the Negro* 1 (January 1904), reprinted in *The Voice of the Negro* (New York: Negro Universities Press, 1969), https://babel.hathitrust.org/cgi/pt?id=uva.x000372425&view=1up&seq=10&q1=keep%20you%20posted.

2. As quoted in Bethany Johnson, "Freedom and Slavery in *The Voice of the Negro*: Historical Memory and African-American Identity, 1904–1907," *Georgia Historical Quarterly* 84, no. 1 (2000): 38.

3. "Martin Luther King Jr. Historic Resource Study—Appendix B: Building Descriptions," National Park Service, October 26, 2002, https://www.nps.gov/parkhistory/online_books/malu/hrs/hrsab.htm.

### SHOTGUN ROW HOUSES

1. "Three Double-Shotgun Houses, 493ABC Auburn Avenue, Historic Structures Report," National Park Service, Cultural Resources, Partnerships and Science Division, Southeast Region. May 2017, http://npshistory.com/publications/malu/hsr-493abc-auburn.pdf.

2. "Double-Shotgun House, 480 Auburn Avenue, Historic Structure Report," National Park Service, Cultural Resources, Partnerships and Science Division, Southeast Region. 2018, http://npshistory.com/publications/malu/hsr-480-auburn.pdf.

## Chapter 2. MLK

### THE KING CENTER

1. "What We Do: King Library and Archives," King Center, accessed December 28, 2023, https://thekingcenter.org/what-we-do/king-library-and-archives/.

2. "Timeline: #DearCoretta," King Center, accessed December 28, 2023, https://timeline.thekingcenter.org/dear-coretta/.

### EBENEZER BAPTIST CHURCH

1. "Social Gospel," Martin Luther King, Jr., Research and Education Institute, Stanford University, accessed December 28, 2023, https://kinginstitute.stanford.edu/social-gospel.

2. "Only One Official Eulogy Was Delivered at Martin Luther King Jr.'s Public Funeral. Read the Full Text Here," *Time*, April 4, 2018, https://time.com/5224875/martin-luther-king-jr-eulogy/.

3. "Only One Official Eulogy Was Delivered at Martin Luther King Jr.'s Public Funeral."

4. Simon Winchester, "From the Archive, 1 July 1974: Martin Luther King's Mother Slain in Church." *The Guardian*, July 1, 2014, https://www.theguardian.com/world/2014/jul/01/martin-luther-kings-mother-slain-in-church-1974.

### COX BROTHERS FUNERAL HOME

1. Gene Kansas, with guest D. L. Henderson, "Alive at Oakland Cemetery," *Sidewalk Radio*, episode 4, January 6, 2011, http://sidewalkradio.com/episodes/single/51.

2. "Famous Residents," Oakland Cemetery, accessed December 28, 2023, https://oaklandcemetery.com/famous-residents/.

3. Benjamin E. Mays, *Dr. Benjamin E. Mays Speaks: Representative Speeches of a Great American Orator* (Lanham, Md.: University Press of America, 2002), 16.

4. Nora McGreevy, "New Legislation Seeks to Protect the U.S.' Historic Black Cemeteries," *Smithsonian Magazine*, December 29, 2020, https://www.smithsonianmag.com/smart-news/legislation-protect-african-american-burial-grounds-passes-senate-180976642/; "Foundation," South-View Cemetery, accessed December 28, 2023, https://southviewcemetery.com/foundation/.

5. Kami Fletcher, "7 Elements of African American Mourning Practices & Burial Traditions." *Talk Death*, February 8, 2021, https://www.talkdeath.com/7-elements-of-african-american-mourning-practices-burial-traditions/.

SOUTHERN CHRISTIAN LEADERSHIP CONFERENCE

1. "SCLC History," Southern Christian Leadership Conference, accessed December 28, 2023, https://nationalsclc.org/about/history/.

2. "Ella Baker," Student Nonviolent Coordinating Committee, accessed December 28, 2023, https://snccdigital.org/people/ella-baker/.

3. Lyndon B. Johnson, "Special Message to Congress: The American Promise, March 15, 1965," in *Public Papers of the Presidents of the United States: Lyndon B. Johnson, 1965* (Washington, D.C.: U.S. Government Printing Office, 1966), 1:281, https://web.archive.org/web/20141128231939/http://www.lbjlib.utexas.edu/johnson/archives.hom/speeches.hom/650315.asp.

## Chapter 3. Dobbs

THE PRINCE HALL MASONIC LODGE

1. "(1797) Prince Hall Speaks to the African Lodge, Cambridge, Massachusetts," *Black Past*, January 22, 2007, https://www.blackpast.org/african-american-history/1797-prince-hall-speaks-african-lodge-cambridge-massachusetts/.

BIG BETHEL AFRICAN METHODIST EPISCOPAL (AME) CHURCH

1. Gregory D. Coleman, "*Heaven Bound*," *New Georgia Encyclopedia*, last modified August 22, 2013, https://www.georgiaencyclopedia.org/articles/arts-culture/heaven-bound/.

JOHN LEWIS HERO MURAL

1. Gene Kansas, with guest John Lewis, "Freedom: The City from Civil War to Civil Rights," *Sidewalk Radio*, episode 22, July 27, 2012, http://sidewalkradio.com/episodes/single/27#.YgaKQ-7MI6E.

BUTLER STREET YMCA

1. John B. Smith Jr., "Remembering Atlanta Business Icon Jesse Hill, Jr.," *Atlanta Inquirer*, December 18, 2012, https://atlinq.com/remembering-atlanta-business-icon-jesse-hill-jr/.

## Chapter 4. Auburn at Piedmont

CITIZENS TRUST BANK

1. Lyndon B. Johnson, "The War on Poverty, March 1964," in *Public Papers of the Presidents of the United States: Lyndon B. Johnson, 1963–1964* (Washington: U.S. Government Printing Office, 1965), 380, 378, https://sourcebooks.fordham.edu/mod/1964johnson-warpoverty.asp.

### *ATLANTA DAILY WORLD* BUILDING

1. Alan Sverdlik, "*Atlanta Daily World*," *New Georgia Encyclopedia*, last modified March 18, 2021, https://www.georgiaencyclopedia.org/articles/arts-culture/atlanta-daily-world/.

2. "Girl Scout History," Girl Scouts, accessed February 18, 2024, https://www.girlscouts.org/en/discover/about-us/history.html.

3. Erin Blakemore, "Girl Scouting Was Once Segregated," *Smithsonian Magazine*, February 21, 2017, https://www.smithsonianmag.com/smart-news/girl-scouting-was-once-segregated-180962208/.

4. "Poinciana Offers Entertainment Tops," *Atlanta Daily World*, November 18, 1945.

5. Stanley Dance, *The World of Count Basie* (New York: Scribner's, 1980), quoted in Steven Cerra, "Count Basie by Alun Morgan—Part 4," Jazz Profiles, November 6, 2018, https://jazzprofiles.blogspot.com/2018/11/count-basie-by-alun-morgan-part-4.html.

6. Colin Larkin, ed., *The Guinness Who's Who of Blues*, 2nd ed. (London: Guinness, 1995), 189.

## Chapter 5. Edgewood and Downtown

### DIXIE COCA-COLA BOTTLING COMPANY PLANT

1. "Book Tells of Stern Maddox Order on Marchers," *New York Times*, July 6, 1968, https://timesmachine.nytimes.com/timesmachine/1968/07/06/76951266.html?pageNumber=19.

### HERREN'S

1. Both quotes from "Herren's Restaurant: An Urban Story," Georgia Tech: Building Memories, accessed December 27, 2023, https://leading-edge.iac.gatech.edu/building-memories/herrens-restaurant-an-urban-story/.

2. Ibid.

### NATIONAL CENTER FOR CIVIL AND HUMAN RIGHTS

1. Lisa George, "Andrew Young on 1996 Olympics: 'We Were Working Together.'" WABE, July 21, 2016, https://www.wabe.org/andrew-young-1996-olympics-we-were-working-together/.

## Chapter 6. Old Fourth Ward

### KING MEMORIAL MARTA STATION

1. "Homes at the Park: Beautiful Residences That Make Inman Park an Ideal Home Place," *Atlanta Constitution*, March 26, 1896.

# Additional Reading

## Chapter 1. The Birth Home Block


### CHARLES LINCOLN HARPER HOUSE

"Charles Lincoln Harper." City of Atlanta Mayor's Office of Cultural Affairs. Accessed December 27, 2023. https://www.ocaatlanta.com/public_art/charles-lincoln-harper/.

"535 Auburn Avenue, NE Historic Structure Report." National Park Service, Cultural Resources, Partnerships and Science Division, Southeast Region. August 2019. http://npshistory.com/publications/malu/hsr-535-auburn.pdf.

Walker, Vanessa Siddle. *The Lost Education of Horace Tate: Uncovering the Hidden Heroes Who Fought for Justice in Schools*. New York: New Press, 2018.

"Welcome Message." Big Bethel AME Church. Accessed December 27, 2023. https://www.bigbethelame.org/Welcome-Message.

### HAMILTON HOWELL HOUSE

Caldwell, Arthur Bunyan. "Alexander Daniel Hamilton." In *History of the American Negro and His Institutions, Georgia Edition*, 86–88. Atlanta: A. B. Caldwell, 1917. https://babel.hathitrust.org/cgi/pt?id=hvd.32044015579857&view=1up&seq=106&q1=Alexander%20hamilton.

Craig, Robert M. "Alexander Hamilton and Son." *New Georgia Encyclopedia*. Last modified August 7, 2013. https://www.georgiaencyclopedia.org/articles/arts-culture/alexander-hamilton-and-son.
"A Walking Tour of Sweet Auburn in Atlanta." NBC News. May 30, 2006. https://www.nbcnews.com/id/wbna12923155.

#### BRYANT-GRAVES HOUSE

"Bryant Preparatory Institute." VoiceMap. Accessed December 27, 2023. https://voicemap.me/tour/atlanta-georgia/exploring-sweet-auburn-a-civil-rights-history-tour/sites/bryant-preparatory-institute-3.
"Freedom's Journal, the First U.S. African-American Owned Newspaper." Wisconsin Historical Society. Accessed December 27, 2023. https://www.wisconsinhistory.org/Records/Article/CS4415.
Pfingsten, Bill. "Bryan-Graves House." Historical Marker Database. Accessed December 27, 2023. https://www.hmdb.org/m.asp?m=73179.

#### FIRE STATION NO. 6

"Fire Station No. 6—A Brief History." National Park Service, May 19, 2015. https://www.nps.gov/malu/learn/historyculture/fsn6-brief-history.htm.
Sams, Douglas. "Atlanta's Best Architecture: Fire Station No. 6, MLK District (SLIDESHOW)." *Atlanta Business Chronicle*, February 17, 2016. https://www.bizjournals.com/atlanta/real_talk/2016/02/atlantas-best-architecture-fire-station-no-6-mlk.html.

### Chapter 2. MLK

#### THE KING CENTER

Eskew, Glenn T. "King Center." *New Georgia Encyclopedia*. Last modified January 10, 2014. https://www.georgiaencyclopedia.org/articles/history-archaeology/king-center.
"Georgia: Martin Luther King, Jr. National Historical Park." National Park Service. Last updated June 18, 2020. https://www.nps.gov/places/georgia-martin-luther-king-jr-national-historical-park.htm.
The King Center. Accessed December 27, 2023. https://thekingcenter.org/.

#### OUR LADY OF LOURDES

"History." Our Lady of Lourdes Catholic Church. Accessed December 27, 2023. https://lourdesatlanta.org/history/.
"Our Lady of Lourdes Catholic Church." Georgia Historical Society. Accessed December 27, 2023. https://georgiahistory.com/ghmi_marker_updated/our-lady-of-lourdes-catholic-church-atlantas-first-african-american-catholic-church/.

#### WHEAT STREET BAPTIST CHURCH

Du Bois, W. E. B. *The Negro Church*. 1903. Eugene, Ore.: Cascade Books, 2011.

Hatfield, Edward A. "William Holmes Borders." *New Georgia Encyclopedia*. Last modified August 24, 2020. https://www.georgiaencyclopedia.org/articles/arts-culture/william-holmes-borders-1905-1993.

"Our Story." Wheat Street Baptist Church. Accessed December 27, 2023. https://www.wearewheatstreet.org/our-story.

"Wheat Street Tower." TSW. Accessed December 27, 2023. https://www.tsw-design.com/portfolio-items/wheat-street-tower-and-annex-building/.

#### SOUTHERN CHRISTIAN LEADERSHIP CONFERENCE

"Behind the Masonic Symbols: The Cornerstone." Free and Accepted Masons, Grand Lodge of Ohio. Accessed December 27, 2023. https://www.freemason.com/behind-masonic-symbols-cornerstone/.

Cooksey, Elizabeth C. "Southern Christian Leadership Conference." *New Georgia Encyclopedia*. Last modified October 26, 2012. https://www.georgiaencyclopedia.org/articles/arts-culture/southern-christian-leadership-conference-sclc/.

Peters, Andy. "$10.2 Million Project to Restore Home of SCLC, MLK's Office." *Atlanta Journal Constitution*, March 1, 2021. https://www.ajc.com/news/atlanta-news/102-million-project-to-restore-home-of-sclc-mlks-office/JTLKP6KGVJETDIVSRCBFBXG2MA/.

"Prince Hall Masonic Grand Lodge." Atlanta History Center. Accessed February 18, 2024. https://www.atlantahistorycenter.com/prince-hall-masonic-grand-lodge/.

"Prince Hall Masonic Lodge." Georgia Tech: Building Memories. Accessed December 27, 2023. https://leading-edge.iac.gatech.edu/building-memories/prince-hall-masonic-lodge/.

"Protecting the Cultural Resources." National Park Service. Last updated October 8, 2020. https://www.nps.gov/malu/protecting-the-cultural-resources.htm.

Ransby, Barbara. *Ella Baker and the Black Freedom Movement: A Radical Democratic Vision*. Chapel Hill: University of North Carolina Press, 2003.

Richards, Raymond C. "Black History Month 1994: Empowering Afro-American Organizations: Present and Future (History of Selected African-American Organizations)." Defense Equal Opportunity Management Institute. October 1993. https://www.defenseculture.mil/Portals/90/Observance%20Archives/BHM/2002-2015/PRES-1994BHM.pdf?ver=2020-06-01-100205-420.

"Who Was Ella Baker?" Ella Baker Center for Human Rights. Accessed December 27, 2023. https://ellabakercenter.org/who-was-ella-baker/.

## Chapter 3. Dobbs


### THE PRINCE HALL MASONIC LODGE

"The Madame CJ Walker Museum." Accessed February 18, 2024. www.madamecjwalkermuseum.com.

"Prince Hall Masonic Grand Lodge." Atlanta History Center. Accessed February 18, 2024. https://www.atlantahistorycenter.com/prince-hall-masonic-grand-lodge/.

### JOHN WESLEY DOBBS PLAZA

"Biography of Charles L. Harper." Atlanta Public Schools. Accessed December 27, 2023. https://www.atlantapublicschools.us/Page/60053.

Hatfield, Edward A. "Auburn Avenue." *New Georgia Encyclopedia*. Last modified September 24, 2020. https://www.georgiaencyclopedia.org/articles/counties-cities-neighborhoods/auburn-avenue-sweet-auburn.

"Through His Eyes." City of Atlanta Mayor's Office of Cultural Affairs. Accessed December 27, 2023. https://ocaatlanta.com/archives/public_art/through-his-eyes.

### ODD FELLOWS BUILDING AND ANNEX

"Atrium on Sweet Auburn." Atlanta Downtown. Accessed December 27, 2023. https://www.atlantadowntown.com/go/atrium-on-sweet-auburn.

"1912 Facts and Trivia." Association for Education in Journalism and Mass Communication. https://web.archive.org/web/20120509044228/http://www.aejmc100.org/trivia/.

"Odd Fellows Building." Atlanta History Center. Accessed December 27, 2023. https://album.atlantahistorycenter.com/digital/collection/athpc/id/83.

"Oddfellows Building." Easements Atlanta. Accessed December 27, 2023. http://easementsatlanta.org/portfolio-item/oddfellows-building/.

"Odd Fellows Building and Atrium." Library of Congress. Accessed December 27, 2023. https://www.loc.gov/pictures/item/ga0209/.

Poole, Shelia. "A Testament to Black Businesses: Odd Fellows Building Observes Centennial." *Atlanta Journal-Constitution*, May 1, 2013. https://www.ajc.com/news/local/testament-black-businesses-odd-fellows-building-observes-centennial/KZOTWB0gR8q2JV2szDe7mJ/.

Thomas, Velma Maia. "Centennial Celebration: The Odd Fellows Buildings." *Atlanta Daily World*, April 29, 2013. https://atlantadailyworld.com/2013/04/29/centennial-celebration-the-odd-fellows-buildings/.

#### BIG BETHEL AFRICAN METHODIST EPISCOPAL (AME) CHURCH

Carmolingo, Nicole. "Big Bethel African Methodist Episcopal Church." *New Georgia Encyclopedia*. Last modified July 15, 2020. https://www.georgiaencyclopedia.org/articles/arts-culture/big-bethel-african-methodist-episcopal-church/.

Coleman, Gregory D. "*Heaven Bound*." *New Georgia Encyclopedia*. Last modified August 22, 2013. https://www.georgiaencyclopedia.org/articles/arts-culture/heaven-bound/.

Coleman, Gregory D. *We're Heaven Bound!: Portrait of a Black Sacred Drama*. Athens: University of Georgia Press, 1992.

"History." Morris Brown College. https://morrisbrown.edu/history/. Accessed December 27, 2023.

#### BUTLER STREET YMCA

Davis, Townsend. *Weary Feet, Rested Souls: A Guided History of the Civil Rights Movement*. New York: W. W. Norton, 1999.

Lamar, Harold D. "Members of Omega Psi Phi Create the Hungry Club Forum of the Butler YMCA." *Atlanta Inquirer*, November 18, 2020. https://atlinq.com/members-of-omega-psi-phi-create-the-hungry-club-forum-of-the-butler-ymca/.

Mapp, Wesley. "They Close the Butler Street YMCA and What Will Blacks DO to Save it!" *Patch*, December 13, 2012. https://patch.com/georgia/cascade/bp—they-close-the-butler-street-ymca-and-what-will-b9b5b361225.

"Selena Sloan Butler." *Georgia Women of Achievement*. Accessed December 27, 2023. https://www.georgiawomen.org/selena-sloan-butler.

Smith, Kimberly. "Jesse Hill: A Life in Photos." *Atlanta Journal-Constitution*. Accessed December 27, 2023. https://www.ajc.com/news/local-obituaries/jesse-hill-life-photos/CbeYNQMvno7RXfnbn4NwDO/.

Smith, John B., Jr. "Remembering Atlanta Business Icon Jesse Hill, Jr." *Atlanta Inquirer*, December 18, 2012. https://atlinq.com/remembering-atlanta-business-icon-jesse-hill-jr/.


## Chapter 4. Auburn at Piedmont


#### THE ROYAL PEACOCK

Image. Library of Congress. Accessed December 27, 2023. https://tile.loc.gov/storage-services/service/pnp/habshaer/ga/ga0200/ga0211/photos/056731pv.jpg.

"Juneteenth: Royal Peacock." Atlanta History Center. Accessed February 18, 2024. https://www.atlantahistorycenter.com/programs-events/public-programs/juneteenth/royal-peacock/.

"186 Auburn Avenue." Library of Congress. Accessed December 27, 2023. https://www.loc.gov/resource/hhh.ga0211.photos/?sp=7.

O'Neill, Connor Towne. "Nightclubbing: Royal Peacock." Red Bull Music Academy. August 18, 2016. https://daily.redbullmusicacademy.com/2016/08/royal-peacock-nightclubbing-feature.

Ruggieri, Melissa. "The 'Queen of Soul,' Aretha Franklin, Dies at 76." *Atlanta Journal-Constitution*, August 16, 2018. https://www.ajc.com/blog/music/the-queen-soul-aretha-franklin-dies/lUdi4s865m8XWKhtRadQKJ/.

Waterhouse, Jon. "5 Places That Defined Atlanta's Culture as You Know It." *Atlanta Journal-Constitution*, March 15, 2016. https://www.ajc.com/places/places-that-defined-atlanta-culture-you-know/1pGgWlmVnISiHOQcPsblnL/.

### CITIZENS TRUST BANK

"Black History Month and Credit Unions." New Orleans Firemen's Federal Credit Union. February 14, 2022. https://www.noffcu.org/articles/article/2022/02/black-history-month-and-credit-unions.

Caro, Robert A. *The Years of Lyndon Johnson*. 4 vols. New York: Penguin Random House, 1982–2012.

"Citizens Trust Company." Digital Library of Georgia. "https://dlg.usg.edu/record/gsu_lane_4503?canvas=0&x=551&y=618&w=4258.

"Economic Opportunity Act." *Britannica*. Accessed December 27, 2023. https://www.britannica.com/topic/Economic-Opportunity-Act.

"Great Society." History.com. Last updated August 28, 2018. https://www.history.com/topics/1960s/great-society.

Lewis, Willard C. "Citizens Trust Bank." *New Georgia Encyclopedia*. Last modified October 30, 2021. https://www.georgiaencyclopedia.org/articles/business-economy/citizens-trust-bank.

"Our Legacy." Citizens Trust Bank. Accessed December 27, 2023. https://ctbconnect.com/history/.

Willis, Haisten. "Nearly 100 Years Old, Black-Owned Citizens Trust Bank Champions Homeownership, Development." *Atlanta Journal-Constitution*, February 18, 2020. https://www.ajc.com/business/committed-the-community/vxca8AuhxALRadmZJ5UyfN/.

Wilson, Kwanjai. "Kenley's, a Place to Remember." Diversity in Downtown, April 14, 2016. https://kwanjaiwilson.wordpress.com/2016/04/14/kenleys-a-place-to-remember/.

### *ATLANTA DAILY WORLD* BUILDING

Sverdlik, Alan. "*Atlanta Daily World.*" *New Georgia Encyclopedia*. Last modified March 18, 2021. https://www.georgiaencyclopedia.org/articles/arts-culture/atlanta-daily-world/.

### 100 BLACK MEN OF AMERICA

*Atlanta City Directory for 1899*. Atlanta: Atlanta City Directory Co., 1899. https://archive.org/details/atlantacitydirec1899vvbu/page/126/mode/2up.

"Martin Luther King, Jr., National Historic Site: Historic Resource Study." National Park Service, Southeast Division, August 1993. http://npshistory.com/publications/malu/hrs.pdf.

"Nathaniel R. Goldston, III." HistoryMakers. Accessed December 27, 2023. https://www.thehistorymakers.org/biography/nathaniel-r-goldston-iii.

"Our History, Our Foundation and Its Recognizable Impact." 100 Black Men of America. Accessed December 27, 2023. https://100blackmen.org/our-history/.

### SOUTHERN SCHOOL BOOK BUILDING

Strahorn, Deborah, Marcy Breffle, and Adina Langer. "Apex and Oakland: Partnership for Black History Education, Part 1." National Council on Public History, May 21, 2019. https://ncph.org/history-at-work/apex-and-oakland-part-1/.

### CENTENNIAL HALL

"Centennial Hall." Georgia State University. Accessed December 27, 2023. https://events.gsu.edu/explore-event-spaces/centennial-hall/.

Chenault, Wesley. "Herman J. Russell." *New Georgia Encyclopedia*. Last modified September 17, 2020. https://www.georgiaencyclopedia.org/articles/business-economy/herman-j-russell-1930-2014/.

"H. J. Russell Center for Entrepreneurship." Georgia State University. Accessed December 27, 2023. https://eni.gsu.edu/hjrussell-center-for-entrepreneurship/.

"Norris Bumstead Herndon." Herndon Foundation. Accessed December 27, 2023. https://www.theherndonfoundation.org/biography/norris-bumstead-herndon/.

"Russell Innovation Center for Entrepreneurs." Russell Center. Accessed December 27, 2023. https://russellcenter.org/.

Saporta, Maria. "Atlanta Life Selling Downtown Headquarters to Georgia State." *Atlanta Business Chronicle*, May 4, 2012. https://www.bizjournals.com/atlanta/print-edition/2012/05/04/atlanta-life-selling-downtown.html.

### AUBURN AVENUE RESEARCH LIBRARY

"Auburn Avenue Research Library." Georgia Tech: Building Memories. https://leading-edge.iac.gatech.edu/building-memories/auburn-avenue-research-library/.

## Chapter 5. Edgewood and Downtown


### THE CURB MARKET

Craig, Robert M. "A. Ten Eyck Brown." *New Georgia Encyclopedia*. Last modified December 7, 2016. https://www.georgiaencyclopedia.org/articles/arts-culture/a-ten-eyck-brown-1878-1940/.

Kansas, Gene, with guests Pam Joiner, Richard Laub, Tim Borchers, Steven Smith, and Keith Schroeder. "The Curb Market." *Sidewalk Radio*, episode 35, August 26, 2013. http://sidewalkradio.com/episodes/single/93.

"Yesterday." Municipal Market. Accessed December 27, 2023. https://municipalmarketatl.com/about/yesterday/.

### DIXIE COCA-COLA BOTTLING COMPANY PLANT

"The Birth of a Refreshing Idea: Coca-Cola History." Coca-Cola Company. Accessed December 27, 2023. https://www.coca-colacompany.com/company/history/the-birth-of-a-refreshing-idea.

Burns, Rebecca. "Funeral." *Atlanta*, April 1, 2008. https://www.atlantamagazine.com/great-reads/mlk-funeral-1968/.

"Dixie Coca-Cola Bottling Company Plant." City of Atlanta, Ga. Accessed December 27, 2023. https://www.atlantaga.gov/government/departments/city-planning/office-of-design/urban-design-commission/dixie-coca-cola-bottling-company-plant.

"Dixie Coca-Cola Bottling Company Plant." National Park Service. Accessed February 18, 2024. https://web.archive.org/web/20090131023405/http://tps.cr.nps.gov/nhl/detail.cfm?ResourceId=1723&ResourceType=Building.

"The History of 125 Edgewood Avenue." Baptist Collegiate Ministries at GSU. Accessed December 27, 2023. https://www.bcmgsu.org/history/.

"International Civil Rights Walk of Fame: Ivan Allen." National Park Service. Accessed December 27, 2023. https://www.nps.gov/features/malu/feat0002/wof/ivan_allen.htm.

National Historic Landmark Nomination for Dixie Coca-Cola Bottling Company Plant. Submitted September 5, 2009. National Park Service. https://npgallery.nps.gov/NRHP/GetAsset/NHLS/77000428_text.

### HERREN'S

"Herren's Restaurant: An Urban Story." Georgia Tech: Building Memories. Accessed December 27, 2023. https://leading-edge.iac.gatech.edu/building-memories/herrens-restaurant-an-urban-story/.

"History." Theatrical Outfit. Accessed December 27, 2023. https://www.theatricaloutfit.org/about-us/history/.

Negri, Ed. *Herren's: An Atlanta Landmark*. Roswell, Ga.: Roswell Publishing, 2005.

Negri, Steven. "Ye Olde Herren's Restaurant." Adventures Before and After, August 18, 2015. https://stevenegri.wordpress.com/2015/08/18/ye-olde-herrens-restaurant/.

#### NATIONAL CENTER FOR CIVIL AND HUMAN RIGHTS

"About the Center." National Center for Civil and Human Rights. Accessed December 27, 2023. https://www.civilandhumanrights.org/about-the-center/.

"A Case Study in Georgia's Business History: 1996 Summer Olympic Games." Georgia Historical Society. Accessed December 27, 2023. https://georgiahistory.com/wp-content/uploads/2018/02/GWCCA-12-4-17.pdf.

"National Center for Civil and Human Rights / HOK + The Freelon Group (Now part of Perkins+Will)." *Arch Daily*. July 22, 2015. https://www.archdaily.com/770551/national-center-for-civil-and-human-rights-the-freelon-group-architects-plus-hok.

## Chapter 6. Old Fourth Ward

#### ABOUT O4W

Severance, Margaret. *Official Guide to Atlanta: Including Information of the Cotton States and International Exposition*. Atlanta: Foot and Davies, 1895.

#### KING MEMORIAL MARTA STATION

Giesberg, Judith. *Army at Home: Women and the Civil War on the Northern Home Front*. Chapel Hill: University of North Carolina Press, 2012.

"History of Metropolitan Atlanta Rapid Transit Authority." Wikipedia. Accessed February 18, 2024. https://en.wikipedia.org/wiki/History_of_Metropolitan_Atlanta_Rapid_Transit_Authority.

Kansas, Gene, with guests Ted Freeman, Brian Bell, Heather Alhadeff, and Paul Grether. "MARTA Art, Architecture and History." *Sidewalk Radio*, episode 10, July 14, 2011. http://sidewalkradio.com/episodes/single/24.

"Southwest Atlanta and the Original Streetcars." Atlanta BeltLine, April 16, 2015. https://beltline.org/2015/04/16/southwest-atlanta-and-the-original-streetcars/.

Wells, Ida B. *Crusade for Justice: The Autobiography of Ida B. Wells*. Chicago: University of Chicago Press, 1970.

#### OLD FOURTH WARD WATER TOWER

Leland, John. "A Tale of Two Downtowns." *New York Times*, October 12, 2000. https://www.nytimes.com/2000/10/12/garden/a-tale-of-two-downtowns-after-worst-of-times-building-for-the-best.html.

Minor, Stephanie. "Just What Is That Tower in the Old Fourth Ward?" *Atlanta*, November 14, 2013. https://www.atlantamagazine.com/article/just-what-is-that-tower-in-the-old-fourth-ward/.

Moore, Jacqueline M. "Booker T. Washington's 1895 Atlanta Exposition Speech (1908 Recreation)." Library of Congress. https://www.loc.gov/static/programs/national-recording-preservation-board/documents/BookerT.pdf.

Washington, Booker T. "The Atlanta Exposition Address." National Park Service. Last updated July 16, 2021. https://www.nps.gov/bowa/learn/historyculture/atlanta1-1.htm.